P9-DJK-283

Collected Poems of
Abbie Huston Evans

Collected Poems
Abbie Huston Evans

University of
Pittsburgh Press

ISBN 0–8229–3208–3
Library of Congress Catalogue Card Number 78–124447
Copyright © 1950, 1952, 1953, 1956, 1959, 1960, 1961, 1966, 1970
  by Abbie Huston Evans
Henry M. Snyder & Co., Inc.
Manufactured in the United States of America

Publication of this
book has been made
possible by grants
to the International
Poetry Forum from
the Commonwealth of
Pennsylvania Council
on the Arts,
the Settlement Music
School and the
College Settlement
of Philadelphia,
and the National
Endowment for the Arts,
Washington, D.C.

To Hester

Contents

The Bright North (1938)

I

Foreword to *Outcrop*

THESE are the poems of one more deeply and more constant-
ly aware than most people are, of the many voices and
faces of lively nature. More than once, in reading them, you
will find yourself stock-still before some object with which you
have rubbed elbows all your life but which you have never
truly seen until that moment; you will learn how *"water-
velvet furs the mullein leaf"*; hear *"the cricket ring his little
bell of glass"*; and

> *Through the blazing mica grains by a road well known*
> *Watch the small red spider running down the stone.*

Those persons who never long to be in the country except
when it is insufferably hot in the city will not, I think, be
greatly attracted to this book. For it will be to them like a book
in a language with which they are unacquainted. And whereas
in some poetry—the poetry of Poe, for instance, of Baudelaire
and of Verlaine—there is a sensuous music so compelling as to
set beating the hearts even of those to whom the meaning is
not clear, in these poems of Miss Evans the music and the
meaning are so intermixed as to be inseparable; these verses
sing partly to the ear and partly to the mind.

Here is no wind from a garden of honeysuckle and roses
wafted at dusk into a room where someone plays Chopin from
memory. The fragrance given out by these pages is as the fra-
grance of some sturdy roadside weed which one has known
since childhood without ever having guessed that it smelled
at all; some day one bends above it and is startled into a cry
by its delicate and subtle odor. Beauty to this poet is a hardy
goddess, one of those

> *Lean-fingered and rock-clinging things,*
> *Bitter-berried, far from springs*
> *Of sweet water, wringing up*
> *Moisture from the rock's own cup;*

a creature nourished *"on the mountain's flinty bread,"* and *"on seed-pods left above the snow."*

Read these poems too swiftly, or only once, and your heart may still be free of them. Read them again, with care, and they will lay their hands upon you.

EDNA ST. VINCENT MILLAY

Outcrop (1928)   I

Salvage

I heard the crickets all about,
Drunk with sunshine, shout and shout.
Mountain-cranberry by the ledge,
Fingering the sun-warmed edge,
Fed its berries round and red
On the mountain's flinty bread,
And the hazel crooked its stalk
To nurse its nuts against the rock.
In the seam—O fair, fair, fair!—
Feathered grasses shone like hair;
Up there on the mountain-side
They had yielded seed, and died.

—This much I was quick to mark,
Against the winter and the dark.

The Tamarack Tree

"Make a true song of me!" the tamarack cried
At the far edge of the pasture (would I could!);
"Make a true song!"—and would not be denied,
Crying aloud from the outskirts of the wood.

Here was no beauty to waylay the eye;
That spidery green, that meagre rough-scaled girth,
Cut a poor figure spread out on the sky:
But how life filled it, climbing up from earth!

"Make a true song!"—I knew it would not do
To forge one word—"A true song, if you can:
Make such a song as I should make of you
If I, a tree, should sing about a man!"

The Mountains

Wind blows upon them, salt-edged from the ocean,
Rain beats upon them, blackening the stone,
Frost heaves the ledges with obscure commotion,
And the hilltops bleach like bone.

Dwindling mountains are they on a dwindling planet,
These that look so solid, these that show so fair;
Wind and rain and frost and hail set tooth to the granite,
It wastes like smoke into air.

Though they now are passing like a slow word spoken,
In the inch of time wherein man stands alone
He sees their rock-knees holding, sees their flanks unbroken,
And his heart drinks strength from the stone.

Yet they are at best but a short-lived generation,
Such as stars must laugh at as they journey forth.
Think of old Orion, that great constellation,
And the Dipper all alone in the north!

The Moment of Beauty

Up through the mud and gravel beauty climbs
To light plain things of earth in sun and wet,
Till what we must have passed a thousand times
We some day see, and never can forget!
Strange how the thousand times fade out at last
And leave the one time when our eyes could see—
How beauty with a touch rubs out the past,
And sets a new mark up for memory.
A boulder beautiful beyond belief,
Witch-hazel blossoms bitten by the cold,
Touched with a sudden shining bright and brief,
Make pictures that we see till we are old;
Ay, what has once been a transfigured thing
Halts us, long after, with remembering.

Ragged Mountain

The fresh young maple leaves put up flat palms
To keep the sun out, but it came through chinks;
And everything in the green-lighted woods
That had no color of its own,—the tree-trunks,
Dead leaves bleached into paper by the rain,
And rocks that nosed up through the forest litter—
Where the sun fell, showed hints of amethyst.
It was as though someone in passing through
The woods that morning had spilled wine in splotches
Along the path, and stained the gray with purple.
Only, of course, no stain is like live sunlight;
Where it lay upon the ground, the leaves and stones
Swam in faint splendor as if under water;
Something was in between that held me off,—
They might as well have been in the bed of a brook,
Taking the tinge of water sliding over.

Here is a strange thing: sky and rock can feed
The spirit of a man as bread his body;
We take up and combine and give out beauty
Under new forms, as plants do what they feed on
(Look at gray dust, and then at larkspur blooms!).
And so it was, the morning that I tell of.
For while I watched it, unaccountably
The baffling, beautiful, unsteady sunlight
Went over into—shall I say, assurance?
Slipped from the outer world of trees and rocks
Into a dimmer place than a green forest,
Where thinking makes a darker shade than trees.

Sea Fog

The world's a ten-rod circle; hills are gone,
Unless this floor of scrub and meadowsweet,
Slanting to hidden nothing, on and on,
May be a hill—I guess it by my feet.

The fir tree dares not shake or even sigh
For fear of spilling beauty bright as brief;
The silver cobweb scares away the fly,
And water-velvet furs the mullein leaf.

O fog-drops strung on birch like beads on hair!
On each red barberry there hangs a tear.
—What wonder I forget the outer air,
Shut in with a little beauty plain and near?

Here's privacy with weeds, relief from sky,
A hollow in gray space; a place, maybe,
Where one may lay disguises safely by,
And strip to the heart in fog from off the sea.

Juniper

For some twisted reason I
Love what many men pass by,—
Lean-fingered and rock-clinging things,
Bitter-berried, far from springs
Of sweet water, wringing up
Moisture from the rock's own cup,
Or drinking in at every pore
Dew and sea mist, if no more;
All things harsh and slow of root,
Pungent, racy, sparse of fruit,
Heather, gorse, and upland fir,
Lichen, moss,—and juniper!

What are two lean years, or three,
Bantling of Necessity,
Who on stony-breasted earth
Long since learned to thrive on dearth?
Long as ledges, will endure
Your rock-fed green and roots obscure,—
Ay, will batten on the stone
After man is dust and bone.

The Light Upon the Rock

(To E. A. T.)

All the while, as the afternoon wore on,
If I but turned my head, there on the stone
Beside me I saw Poetry like a stain.
The level sun came in through the thin leaves
And lit an angle of the lichened rock
Till it took fire with beauty; I could see
That tenderness was on it like a bloom,
But whether laid upon it, from without,
Or breaking to the surface, from within,
I could not tell; there, anyway, it was,
A kind of holiness plain to the eye.

A moosewood spray growing there in the cleft
Spread to the air its few large perfect leaves,
And wavered now and then as if in thought.
Such rank wild things as grew upon the ledge—
The unkempt grass and clambering huckleberries
Along the top, and here and there in cracks
Burrs of green moss, and tough little rock ferns clinging
Like grim death—knew a thing or two, I felt,
That I could only guess at.—Lichens, too,
Big as my palm, smoke-colored, caught in the middle,
And curling up and out like juiceless flowers
Suckled on granite, piqued me with their silence.

But most of all, that light upon the rock
That made it different somehow from the rest,
As if in some strange way addressed to me,
Made my heart beat whenever I turned and saw it.
I couldn't bring myself to speak of it
Even to you—it was too strictly mine—
(Perhaps some other spot shone out for you)
And yet I think it colored all I said.

This much I knew, (though it was days before
The knowledge cleared itself into a thought):
I could risk myself in the hands of any God
Who could make a light like that upon the rock.

Hill-born

Back to this mold, this matrix whence I came,
I come again.—Like solder where it spills,
My being hardened in among these hills
When God took off my metal from the flame
And poured me out like silver; presently,
My outline fixed forever, I was I,
Stamped by this rocky corner like a die,
Shaped by these five hills and this edge of sea.

Oh, strange how hills and man's heart interlock
Inveterately—how rock can bestow
Its contour on his spirit quick within!
Yet so it is: hill-men have always been
Like nuggets fashioned by their chinks, or snow
Packed in the star-like crevice of a rock.

The Spread Table

(After a verse-pattern of W. H. Davies)

When I see birds whose names I do not know
Light on a tree-top twenty feet below,
And though I am so near them, never care,
But peck at cones, a thousand feet in air;

When I see spruces bitten by the wind
Scaling the cliff without a look behind,
And off at sea across the mountain's face
Behold far-sprinkled islands and blue space;

And when, no longer level, the blue sea
Hangs from the sky like a great tapestry,
Hangs from the sky but keeps its blue unblent,
Let down about, like the side-wall of a tent:—

When I see these things, knowing as I do
I break today's bread and tomorrow's too,
At the spread table of the waves and stones
I feed on beauty as the birds on cones.

Next of Kin

So deaf are we, each unto each,
    So halting is our speech,
I may not hear you when you cry,
I may not answer though I try.

The one I told my naked thought
    Looked past me and forgot;
The day my heart held jubilee
My friend at hand was far from me.

—But what a heart is in a hill
    When a man's own doth fill!
Through the long winter by the sea
The hills fail not to answer me.

And I know trees beside old roads
    Grown broad with sharing loads;
Ledges gone gray with rains and years,
That shame the turbulence of tears.

O sweet the tumult in the grass
    When winds and shadows pass!
But finer tumults deep within
Shake the gray earth, my next of kin!

Revisited

The old bleak house upon the open hill
Above the river pastures is the same;
The sweet incessant wind is singing still
Around the corners,—even so it came,
And swelled and failed, but did not wholly die,
When I, a little maid in gingham, played
About the door and heard the Past blow by.
Here where the patient paths my fathers made
Have well-night faded from these meagre fields,
The foolish fennel lifts a poignant face,
And each spent tree and settling stone wall yields
Remembrance up, so constant is the place.
    Old lanes do not forget; old fields are slow
    To disinherit men the grass-roots know.

I Am Broken of My Rest

I am broken of my rest,
Thinking of the streams that lie
Looped across earth's barren breast
Ten times bluer than the sky,—

Of the hallelujah blue
Of crisped water like a shout,
Now the year is almost through
And the sky diluted out:

Thinking how the thorn-bush stands
In a glitter, bright like hair,
At the edge of pasture-lands.
I must try, now earth is bare,

To forget how garnet shows
On the mountains, and how spruce
Sheds out blue before the snows
In this still time like a truce.

Everywhere the woods are thinned,
Everywhere stiff fingers push,
And the lovely halting wind
Wanders on from bush to bush.

The Bird-Tree

The locust tree, inscrutably,
Wears plumage like a bird;
And where is there another tree
Taloned, beaked, and spurred?

Although it never comes to flight,
Lengthwise one by one
It folds its feathers with the night,
And spreads them with the sun.

Bowers Hill

There all the winds light down to blow
Through the stone wall (I know! I know!)

And sunsets linger. (Oh, to see
One burn behind the canted tree!)

The moon above it—there's a sight
To bring a body out at night;

Silver and shadow shine and blur
Down the slopes of juniper,

Until they break to heather-flower,
And Maine is Scotland for an hour!

—Sometimes at night I raise my head
And see the hill beside my bed;

My feet run up the dew-wet stone,
I stand in starlight all alone!

The Back-Road

Perhaps I needed something gray and brown
And did not know it,—something spent and bare,
That morning on the back-road, in November.
I may have stood in need of something bedded
Like the ledge beside me barnacled with lichen,
With a great wave of juniper breaking on it;
Or darkly needed something straight like cedars,
Black on the traveling cloud-fringe,—something steady,
Like slate-gray mountains in behind bare birches.
Perhaps I needed something bright and scarlet,
Like winter berries on the stone-gray bush
Beside the rock-pile,—something sweet and singing,
Like water in the gutter running down
From springs up in the pasture out of sight.

But if I needed these, I did not know it.
If you had told me that I wanted fulness,
Or life, or God, I should have nodded "Yes";
But not a bush of berries,—not a mountain!
—Yet so it was: fantastic needs like these,
Blind bottom hungers like the urge in roots,
Elbowed their way out, jostling me aside;
A need of steadiness, that caught at mountains,
A need of straightness, satisfied with cedars,
A need of brightness, cozened with a bush.

—Whatever it was I needed, know I found it!
The oak-tree standing with its feet in water
Behind me, with the wind hoarse in its top
Of paper, or the thousand-penciled bushes
Across the road, or alders black with catkins,
Fed no more deeply on the earth than I,—
Nor half so passionately, I must think,
As I, who, rooted in my tracks, appeased

Undreamed-of hungers with unlikeliest food,
The first at hand; amazed to find what sweetness
Can be wrung out of clay and flint,—amazed,
Like a starving man in a swamp, to find what relish
Is hid in grass, and bark, and roots, and acorns.

Past Midnight

I stole from bed to see what cast faint light
Upon my wall in the middle of the night,—
Upon my western wall an hour at least
Before a ray of dawn could streak the east.

And I saw starry night outside, but change
Had come upon it, for the east looked strange;
The Pleiades had pushed themselves too high,
And empty gaps showed in the under sky.

The stars, like drops of water, in my sight
Trembled with beauty made new overnight,
And brimmed and trembled, brimmed but did not fall,
As lovely as the day-star, great and small.

And just above the edge the dying moon
Hung with a planet by it, like to swoon,
Dripping with beauty, fresh-washed from the sea.
(—Oh that alone was sight enough for me!)

—The dying moon that waking had crept out
For a last look when no one was about,
And had surprised me with its candle-light
Upon my wall in the middle of the night.

Cock-Crow

This is how to speed a night,
This is how to hail a day
When the first hair-roots of light
Undermine the dark with gray.

What a tumult loosed on air
By the solitary cock
Seeing day creep up the stair,
Hearing light begin to knock!

Pealing bronze—again—again!
Such a sheaf of distant cheers
As if fifty banded men
Back to back defied the spears!

First Concerns

Better go outdoors now, shut the door on trouble,
Lest if I stay indoors life should bend me double;
Care hides in house corners, but has little use
For a hummock pasture full of sun-burnt spruce.

It is high time I found out one or two things: whether
Lambkill is blooming like a flowerier heather;
Whether after all this rain green-white bells are set
Thick on high bush blueberry like wild mignonette.

Better stub my feet on roots, let the bronze-green fly
Sun itself upon my hand imperturbably;
Through the blazing mica grains by a road well-known
Watch the small red spider running down the stone.

Windfalls

I filled my pail and looked around:
Apples littered all the ground,
Pale, bright, up-ended, twig and stem
Snatched from the tree along with them,
Brought down from swinging overhead
To lie with slugs and snails instead.

I filled my pail, I straightened up,
I drank the morning like a cup;
Diminished sunlight flooding in
Showed how leaves were getting thin,
And the wind that whipped my hair
Blew trees beautiful and bare.

I saw a nest out on a bough
I had never seen till now;
Saw the paleness of the sky
Brushed with white, saw leaves blow by
Gold and russet in a shoal
To heap the gully like a bowl;
I saw the poplar saplings lurch,
Saw gold tags spinning on the birch,
Saw the tamarack tossing free,—
And knew them of one piece with me!

Out whirled my heart and down the gale
Like one more leaf set free to sail.
I was a note like A or G
In a rising harmony;
"In this universe I fit"—
I never was so sure of it!
All my tangled lines slid free
And lay parallel in me:

"O golden world, you change and fly,
And so do I—and so do I!
At one beneath, too deep to mark,
Our roots go twining in the dark;
And, all in one, we slip, we move,
Together down this shining groove
Toward that hid Outlet, that sure Whole,
That shall include us, clod and soul!"

II

The Shadow

Still I quake when I recall
A vine's shadow on a wall,
Of such beauty that I shrink
From remembering—how think
Of that outline in that place,
Dark on bright before my face!

Liker to the Copy hid
That all leaves are patterned by
Was that shadow where it slid
Back and forth before my eye
Than the green and shining leaf.

Brighter beauty and less brief
Lives in shadow stripped down bare
Than in leaves that wave in air.

Marigold

As I came down the stair,
Unsatisfied, balked here, balked there,
I stood stock-still:
There at the sill
Was all, for once, a heart could hold.
Oh who could guess
Such satin stuff
As marigold
Spread out to the eye of day!
Clear shining orange, bottomless
And burning; nothing left to crave;
Orange to last me to the grave!
    All hunger dropped away,
    Peace swept me like a wave.
    My heart cried, "Here's enough!"

Earthquake in New England

1

Here is a safe spot on earth's slipping crust;
No earthquakes scare New England; now and then
A tremor too remote to shake old trust,—
No more than this in the memory of men.

But if some day a great crack steaming wide,
Should run from Concord down to Salem, say,
With houses flat as cards on either side,
And clouds of brick-dust slow to clear away,

All would be different: for men would know
More than the earth was shaken, past a doubt;
And down the old trust in their hills would go,
Buried so deep no crew could dig it out,

In insubstantial ruin such that wood
And steel and stone could never make it good.

2

Yet out of earthquake and old faith ploughed under,
Up through packed ash there well might push a shoot
Of urgent green belief—Oh thing for wonder!—
So tough a life is hidden in the root;

And though no man, knowing what he would know,
Could then believe as simply as a child
In earth's sure immobility below,
Or be as he had been before that wild

Unprecedented loosening of clamps
That gave a wrench to rock roots (and man's heart),
He might relinquish trust in hills he tramps
To lean down hard on What pries clamps apart.

—Oh green shoot growing up for all to see!
Oh green shoot that in turn might be a tree!

The Old Yellow Shop

In farming country you are sure to find them,
Little gray wooden buildings boarded up,
Astride a stone wall, or lost in a thicket,
With what shut in?—Well, I think if you pried
A warped board free and climbed in through a window,
You might find much the same thing as I found
In the Yellow Shop on my grandfather's farm:

Darkness at first; pencils of steady sunlight
Alive with dust, that slanted in through chinks,
And such a smell of cedar you would know,
Before your eyes grew wide enough to see,
That the place was full of stacks of fragrant shingles.
Then, tattered paper hanging from the wall,
Crude blue, perhaps, and red—brick-red—and brown,
That chocolate-brown the old folks seemed to fancy.
That might be all.

      —Or might not be.
                        For after
I had stood there for a while, held by the quiet,
A sense of ended things grew up about me.
Someone had lived there once,—I think a cobbler;
It was a place where men had come and gone,
Men of my blood, whose names I did not know;
Whose feet had worn the hollow in the threshold
That let the light in underneath the door;
Whose lives had been blown out, one after one,
By the wind of Time, like candles in a row
Set up to be extinguished.—Yet this shell,
The haunt of dead men, still gave back the sun,
And stood up to the hail and sleet of winter.
—I gripped the nearest thing my hand could find,
A cleat someone had hammered to the wall

To help him clamber to the loft above,
And looked out through the window toward the wood-lot.

The shadow of the Shop ran dark across
The field, which but for that lay in the sun
Serene and smiling and inscrutable;
The air was sweet; blackberry and wild aster
Nodded outside the window in the shade,—
Perpetual things, that, springing year by year,
Are old, by repetition, like the sea;
There was a cricket busy in the stubble,
And a flutter of wings in bushes round the corner;
And in the place, the sense of something ended.
I nailed it up and left it there behind me.

And to this day I never pass the Shop,
Off in its corner, with its blinded eye,
With shingles curling loose and flecks of yellow
Still clinging to the silver of the gray,
But I grow insolent with glorying
In lovely life!—O dancing candle-flame,
Not yet blown out by the delaying wind!

Silhouette

The lamp flared in a quick gust.—"Yet," I said,
"You've had a full life, Sarah."—"That depends;
"If you mean busy, I suppose so. Yes.
"What with the old folks—and Aunt Jane—and Mandy."
She took her basket and got up to go,
Her hand a gaunt root wrapped about the handle.
"—Nothing ever took me off my feet.
"That's the whole story.—Well," she said, "good night."

I held the lamp to light her down the path.

Says Life of Youth

I must take this beautiful thing and break it;
It is time I began:
I shall make a better thing of it,
But nothing so beautiful!

—Nothing so beautiful as Youth
Starting at the sting of a lash,
Cheeks bright, chin high, back taut, and eyes ablaze,
Outraged, betrayed, incredulous of pain,
Of whips, of thorn-rods, in a world of gold,
Reaching superbly for the whip to break it!

I must take this beautiful thing and break it;
It is time I began.
I shall make a better thing of it,
But nothing so beautiful:

Nothing so beautiful, alas,
As Youth tasting the whip;
Nothing so beautiful, alas, alas,
As Youth first bitten by thorn!

Wild Apples

Bright in September, bright against the sky,
Bright against mountains, bright against the sea,
Oh acid fruit and worthless! Pass it by.
Oh beautiful and worthless! Let it be.

Yet the birds take these branches for a house,
Wild grape festoons it, binding tart with tart,
And to the end of time unshaken boughs
Are not for us to laugh at, O my heart!

—Unshaken boughs and fruit ungathered yearly
Save by the wind that brings it scattering down
To bruise on rocks, smash open, juicing clearly,
And rot beneath the tree till it is brown.

Out in back pastures known to sheep and cows,
Blind foot-note to a page, they stand apart;
But to the end of time unshaken boughs
Are not for us to laugh at, O my heart!

The Servant of the Prophet

I never read the story but I wonder
About that young man in the Book of Kings,
The servant of the prophet, who is nameless.
—You know the story: how the host of Syria
Compassed the city in the dead of night,
And how the young man cried,—*"Alas, my master,
How shall we do?"—"Open his eyes, Lord!"* cried
The man of God.
        *"And lo, the side of the mountain
Was full of horses and chariots of fire
About Elisha."*

            —What had dropped away?
Did other things look different as the hill?
And did he, I have wondered, ever after,
Look with a beating heart on a bare field,
Remembering what an empty ridge had held?

I ought to know: for I myself have seen
The flaming chariots blazing through the pine
And scrub oak; not in chariot form, perhaps,
Because it wasn't chariots that I needed
To save me at the time; but I have seen
For an instant, reinforcement, just at hand!
And then the scrub oak shutting in again,
And the hot sunshine beating on the pine.

Yes, ten to one, the young man did forget,
Or like as not explained it all away;
Yet sometimes, in broad daylight,—*"What was that!"*

"Was This the Face—?"

Words can be sent no farther. Shut the book.
This is the extreme push that carries over
Outer to inner. We, defenseless, look
At syllables the dust will never cover.

They have a dazzle in them. Shut the book.
Blood pounds. You see, the impossible can be;
And these few words a man's brain reached and took
Will last though England sinks into the sea.

Arc-Light Shadow

On this shining patch of wall
Crinkled like a sunny brook
Behold Motion rise and fall
While I lie awake to look.

Here the blunt twigs meet and flee,
Thrust and counter, swing and sway,
Balancing immutably
As alternate night and day.

Gone are sound and color quite,
Only rhythm now is left
And a sense of dark on bright;
Yet this one bough straitly cleft

Makes report of settling granite
Deep in earth beneath the tree,
Predicates the wheeling planet
Down its circle swinging free.

Borne up on the heaving crest
Of the vast unquiet All,
I lie out and take my rest,
Cosmos scribbling down my wall.

Invocation

Oh make me honest as a fishing village
In the full sun-glare on a northern coast:
As honest as a hill above bare tillage
When leaves are down and cliffs and scars show most!
Edged like a grain of sand, as bleakly angled,
Flashing like mica, wearing no disguise,
Give me clear outlines never blurred or tangled,
And honest being waiting honest eyes.
Then let men love me with the same clean passion
With which they love the earth that does not lie;
And if I change, may it be in real fashion
As a tree does; and when I come to die
May I be like a field or candid down
Through with earth's green and ready next for brown.

Soul's Passing

It was right that a wind was blowing full of sound and might
Over the crusted snow, an hour before the light;
It was right that in the south like a glittering watch should
stand
A marvel of three planets drawn in from either hand:

It was right that three planets together should wait beyond the
tree,
That the horned moon should veer in and join their company:
For he who was going was bearing—unflawed, unsullied,
whole,
And brighter than all three planets—a jewel like a coal.

The Woman

Be tender of her shyness; have a care—
Such beauty may not stay.
Be one who breaks out of a path to spare
A cobweb in the way.

Be harsh as granite with her granite edges;
Here you may meet as foes.
Granite is granite—beat on her with sledges.
She can endure your blows.

Foursquare

Oh beautiful is a clear square of light
On a dark wall in the middle of the night,
Cornered with Truth and run out on the True.
—This is the outline I concede to you.

And when by night that naked silver shines,
I think how I have seen your equal lines,
Buckled by passion, straighten back to true.
—I could have loved you, had they cracked in two!

The Vine

Love is quaint like columbine,
Queer and new like irises
Among moon-faced flowers; a vine
All original, like these.

And it matters not a whit
What it grows on, I am told;
An old shed will do for it,
Or a pillar cased in gold.

So it have, till it be grown,
Something for a trellis,—good!
Old love can climb round its own
Twisted honeysuckle wood.

Ellen

She had achieved a thorny continence
Like a locust tree in winter. When the spring,
Slow-mounting, picked the wards of every sense
And reached that locked-up heart and made it sting,
She gave it at the best but grudging room.
She knew well that the locust, when it yields,
Threshes its leaves by armfuls, hung with bloom
So thick the bees troop in from all the fields.

Trend

It is enough to know that our lines
Which had seemed to run parallel
Indeed tend inward,
By a split-hair's angle
Imperceptibly converging.

Oh remote in time
As the nebula of Andromeda in space
Must be that viewless but indubitable point
Of meeting!
Oh remote in time
As the nebula in space,
But as fixed, as existent.
Wherefore time, transcended, ceases to be,
And the soul with singing
Prepares itself to run out on an infinite projection.

Paradox

If you would have my love you must be single.
If you would hold my love you must be various.
Change not at all! your strong wine must not mingle.
O alter daily! else love were precarious.

Be strange-familiar: be a wood-road, new
On coming back, the sun the other way,
Whereat men stare amazed (as I with you),
And cry, "This tree was not here yesterday!"

Overborne

I who can endure meagreness alone
Bow under an insupportable load;
I am bent by the weight of too much,
I am borne down by the richness of living.
For music plumbs depth below depth
(And under the deepest is depth),
And above me is splendor, and around me is wonder,
Till I know not where I shall turn unless I can find
A hand to catch, an ear to listen, a heart to share.

My burden is the tassel of the willow tree
And the white sleet of beauty on the ground.

Blind Gentians

I saw them under the tree, and angrily cried,
"It is against nature thus to be denied!"
I saw blind buds that God made grow,
Never to do as flowers do, never to blow.

Bees fumbled at them. *(God, I sweat to think*
What bitterness may be for me to drink!)
Bees fumbled at them by the linden tree.
(What can happen to a flower can happen to me!)

Sheep Laurel

I who was young came on a sight
Hard for young eyes, bitter for old:
I saw sheep laurel leaves all tight,
Rolled into pencils by the cold;

Straight down they hung in clusters, tight
Constricted, each a hollow rod;
The bud stood naked up in sight
Below the bloomed-out pod.

Sheep laurel bushes stood in old
Denuded pastures far apart;
I saw them brittle with the cold,
Their life drawn back into their heart.

Matched with the frost; withstanding cold;
Untouched by panic; above grief.
—See how a small bush does; behold
The bleak endurance of a leaf.

Breton Song

Life is too short to love again.
My loaf is given. Come and see:
I have not crumbs to feed a wren,
So full a toll love took of me.

Oh iron chain of loyalty!
In all the marching world of men
There is no other face for me.
Life is too short to love again.

The Burning Hill

The Burning Hill, they call it. Long ago,
A generation since, the coal took fire;
Men fought the flame awhile, but came to know
It ate too deep and crept too slow to tire.

Sometimes at night men wandering on the hill
See small blue-pointed flames play through a crack,
And know the ancient fire is gnawing still
At the hill's core, red eating up the black.

Yet some day will the last black inch be ash
In the last alley burrowing underground,
And the whole hill stand full of clinkered trash,
A burned-out furnace, one great cinder-mound.

—Oh what of buried fires that show no spark,
Burning away a life-time in the dark?

Winter Fare

The birds tug at the stubborn meadow-sweet
Stiff in the snow, until the brown seeds spill;
They make wild-rose hips give them wizened meat,
And pry out pine-pits with a frozen bill.

What though each grass-blade is an icy splinter?
There was a summer not so long ago.
—Men, too, in lean days, like the birds in winter,
Can live on seed-pods left above the snow.

"—Will He Give Him a Stone?"

I pick it up, I turn it over, I scoff.
I never saw a loaf that looked like this,
That weighed so heavy, had a sound like flint.
Crack it; sniff; taste it; can one swallow it?
Is it stone? is it bread? try; can one swallow it?
Yes, a crumb at a time,—a crumb at a time, O God!
Bitter?—Past words; but somehow, strangely, bread!

Glacier-marked

This is the rock the ice ground over. See
Where furrows still run down it in the sun.
There where the raspberry has taken root,
Back in the inconceivable drift of time
Flint like a nail set in the iron shoe
Of a giant ploughed a way across its flesh.

Since then the years have lighted down like wasps,
To be brushed off. But frost with prick and sting
Of diamond wedges, down the old grooves still
Lets itself in; dimly I am aware
Of minute rendings working toward its heart.

Oh unforgotten, unforgettable
While rock has form, the ice—the ice—the ice!
Along those desperate lines of earliest pain
Put on it in the fore-day of the world,
Time yet shall render it to dust again
Before the sun burns out.

Love in Life

With some, it is the brief flare of a match,
Cupped with both hands against a flaw of air,
Or a quick-taken breath.

With some, it is the great blaze of a beacon
Built on a headland
In a storm:
Flattened by blasts,
Dragged sideways by gales,
Roaring upward in lulls;
Spit at by spray,
Licking up sleet,
Climbing on rain,
Blazing all night in the storm!

III

The Back Pasture

The cows crop round the thistles; hardhack thrusts
Its frugal pink up on a stalk that rusts;
The rutted road is overgrown with turf.
It is a meagre pasture; but to me
It is a sea of beauty, a wild sea,—
Against my rock this pasture breaks in surf.

The sorrel leaf beside me, red like blood
With the sun pouring through it, sends a flood
Of song up through me like wind through a thicket.
—Oh inexhaustible earth, the tireless maker!
Here every hummock is a little acre,
Great done in small, a pasture for a cricket.

The Sassafras Upon the Rock

The sassafras upon the rock,
The bushes in the seam,
The moss where edges interlock,
Confront us, sunk in dream.

The fugitive white butterfly
Is as the ancient crow;
Alike they wander in from sky,
Alike, impassive, go.

But silver fish that make a splash,
And ripples sliding under,
Have power to startle like a crash
Of February thunder.

Oblivious to the ticking clock
And us who go and come,
The colored light rows up the rock,
The ant pursues its crumb.

The Great Bull-Thistle

The great bull-thistle, standing up alone,
Prepares to bloom and sends a summons out:
Hearing that purple hail, that trumpet blown,
The butterflies run on it with a shout
Too fine for ears, and cling and crowd and jostle;
The ranging bee finds here the thing he hunts
(Oh would he now could sing out like a throstle!),
And all together batten, seven at once.

The great bull-thistle when the summer dies
Shall send out on the air on lighter wings
A lighter crowd than this, before the eyes
Of crows and woodchucks sharp for other things.
The great bull-thistle, when the winter nips
The pasture, shall be impotent to sting;
The great bull-thistle shall be only strips
Of burnt-out paper in the fire of spring.

Threatening Rain

I knew that rain was coming right away;
I knew it by the birds and by the leaves.
The sky grew darker, clouds let down their gray,
A bird was making sounds like one who grieves.
I raised my head, a crow was lifting his,
For suddenly the thicket was astir:
I left the prostrate sprays of blueberries
Spread out on gray moss in the juniper,
Taking last berries from beneath a tent
Of cobweb glittering with last night's rain,
I saw bright beauty everywhere I went,
—But, cattle-like, I turned back home again,
    Lagging from stone to hummock, dragging slow
    My feet up homeward as the cattle go.

Yarrow

Here is a red field-lily by a stone
All beautiful—all beautiful! Full-blown
The azure chicory rises in the grass
Like a thin puff of smoke no one can pass
Without a trembling. Here is meadow-rue
With silver feet deep in the morning dew.
   —And is this yarrow cluttering underfoot?
   Yes, dingy yarrow bitter to the root!

Hunger

No one of all my line has ever loved
This river so, I swear,
Or found the sun so sweet, or been so moved
By the bliss of breathing air.

This feast of life, for all it is so good,
Is but an alms, and mean.
My hunger prowls afar, and stalks such food
As eyes have never seen.

If I Had Made—

If I had made these pastures by the river
I could not find them better. Here is what
My fingers might have framed, had I been God,—
This slope of green stretched over rock, these firs,
These points, these coves, these ledges, and this inlet.
Even as it is, the sense of gratulation
Is high within me, and impassioned joy
Of the creator.—*"God looked on his work
And saw that it was good."*—Oh joy, joy, joy!
I might be God now, on the Seventh Day.

A Prayer for Less

There is more beauty in this field than one
Should be called on to bear. I shield my eyes
With up-flung arm against the noon-day sun,
And come on fiercer blaze. Like one who lies
Shipwrecked in seaweed lie I in this grass,
A sailor cast up on a perilous shore,
Not knowing what new ills may come to pass,
What beaks to tear him or what tusks to gore.
—Oh terrible is beauty in its power
To slay the unwary! Back of this I see
Hangs the suspended whole; wherefore I cower;
No man may tempt it with impunity.
    One touch to-day would launch it on my head.
    I know at heart I am as good as dead.

Weeds

Weeds need no man's abetting,
It well may be a sin,
But I am all for letting
The worst of all come in:

Hawkweed, that pest pernicious,
(*More orange than a flame!*)
And blue vetch, full as vicious,
(*Too beautiful to tame!*)

Frown now, it is your duty,
Chide me for one who dotes.
I cannot sleep for beauty
Of charlock in the oats.

Under Cover

Rain with the old sound, with the country sough
From fields and meadows overpast and trees
That strip it into whip-lash, I hear now
Beat on this hill and cut about its knees.
Now while the lithe wind turns and springs again
On the spent tree, and rain floods down the glass,
I hear the sounds earth knew before we men
Came on, and shall know after we shall pass.
While ancient rumor rising to a shriek
Comes in to tell of matters we forget,
I am one more of the beasts of the field in bleak
Ecstatic cover, huddled from the wet.
　　So stands the ox, so crouches now the mole,
　　So sits the dry woodpecker in his hole.

Open Hill

I see a whole shower at once.
A rainbow stands propped in the meadow.
The sunset sweeps up on this hill
With no shield but the edge of the world.

This sky is the whole half of heaven.
Clouds drag here in clearing the earth.
The stars are the pricks in a tent
Let down to the ground all about me.

My house stands up on this hill
As bleached as a hollowed-out tree,
A shelter from rain and from snow,
And a hold where the hail cannot come.

Day-End

The shadow lengthens in across the slope,
Leaving the tips of scrub still in the sun;
The cows are going home beneath the cope,
And the bright day is done.
Where the leaf twirls a sidelong shadow flitters,
And full of shrilling life now is the grass;
The songs of birds have sunk to cries and twitters,
The cricket rings his little bell of glass.

Hearing all quiet sounds of evening round me,
Hearing the distant bellow of a steer,
I know though night once more has sought and found me
There is no need to fear.
And though I know the light has reached its bound,
And though I feel a darkening in the sun,
There is such depth of being in this ground
As makes all ending and beginning one.

The Double Rainbow

(Remembering Wordsworth)

The heart that leaped up at a rainbow lies
A thimbleful of dust;
But I should think this sight before my eyes
Would find it through earth's crust:
Ay, call him back from sights no man has seen
And lived, when all is said,
And break the pane of ice run down between
The living and the dead.

Stars

Across the gulf, across the gulf, they burn,
Antares, and Arcturus, and Altair,
Vega and Spica. Everywhere I turn
I see stars netted in the heaven's hair.

In patterns of an arrow, of a crown,
A wain, a jeweled lyre, a flying swan,
Up to the zenith, from the zenith down,
The heavenly procession winds till dawn,

In silence, silence—Sound, grown cricket-shrill,
On that rock-crystal stillness breaks and shatters.
And suddenly the dark road over the hill
Leads nowhere—or nowhere that really matters.

In Dew

I will not snap a thread of cobweb, even,
If I can help it.—Who am I to spill
One spark of blue fire down? When one's in heaven
One well may stand stock-still.

Here foot can ruin more than hand can make
Or heart can dream of.—Stand here on this flint,
And wait until the sun, for Beauty's sake,
Has furled away this glint!

Secret

These vines on the ground contrive without the sun;
And here are hemlock boughs spread out like lace,
And toadstools pushing wanly one by one.
I tell you, this is a most secret place.

The platform of the stump is covered with moss
And hand-high bushes; up from mouldered wood
The sun cajoled this beauty out across
Where pine-pith once in central darkness stood.

I cannot stay—and yet I cannot go.
I envy squirrels—but they too are blind.
I wonder how this place looks in the snow.
I wish I could come on it from behind.

Barnacles

The snail moves on
    With white horns spread
Over each low
    Enchainèd head,
Down anchored life
    To which that snail
Is a bird for speed
    Or a flying sail.

—But now the rock
    Is all astir,
The inch-deep water
    In a blur,
Where stony slots
    Slide open wide
At the loved washing
    Of the tide,
And filmy hands
    Where none have been
Go reaching out
    And sieving in.

What looked like rock
    Is quick like me!
How dim a rushlight
    Life may be—
Love but an opening
    Hinge, and hate
The sudden shutting
    Of a gate!
These shelly men
    But know the sea
For a recurrent
    Certainty,

75

A something welcome,
  Nothing more;
Life is simple
  By the shore.
Life is simple
  In the deep,
A stirring
  Of the fringe of sleep.

The Still River

(Early Morning)

This is incredible. It cannot be.
I'll not believe the evident thing I see
Unless someone confirms it. Better than I
Have been brought down to imbecility.

This river laid out bare may be but seeming,
This waste of beauty, and this fish-hawk screaming;
I see a pasture and a height of sky,
My eyes are open, but I may be dreaming.

I look, and doubt my senses.—Nay, if three
Should swear they saw this beauty which I see,
I should look on with pity at their lie,
Knowing they too were mad, clean daft like me.

Face to Grass

"Put face to grass,
And feel earth turning."
"—*I do! I do!*"
"Your cheeks are burning!"

"*I felt the spring
The great earth gave,
And leaned to westward
Like a wave.*"

"—Now eyes are shut,
Let sight run round
Like grass-fire over
Stubble ground:

"Survey this great ball
Light in space
As the green berry
By your face."

"—*I see me lying
Prone, a speck
Of pure awareness,
Like a fleck*

"*Of mica burning
Terribly
On a cliff's face
Above the sea.*"

The True Lover

This is the naked insurmountable truth:
Two shall not ever meet.
In spite of passion and the dream of youth,
Two still are two, discrete.

Take for your lover the importunate earth,
You shall achieve desire.
In that great meeting is no hint of dearth,
The tinder is the fire.

The Bright North (1938)   I

Time's Citizen

Do things matter still?—They matter:
Cut-shape, color, chime.
By felt things I know I am
The citizen of Time.

Such all but fingerable life
Lets in no doubt at all;
Tied to the stem, I am a leaf
Secure against the fall.

When the day comes I no more flinch
At dawn's edge coming on,
Staggered as by the ice-cap's shift
I'll know that Time is gone.

The Stone-Wall

Obliterated faces
Look up from the stones
When noon inks in the shadows.
Life is in these drones.
Nothing else created
Has such secret eyes;
Dim mouths set as these are
Make no cries.

Dwellers underground
Dragged up to the air
Lie out and plot together
Against alien glare,
Back to darkness sinking
At a pace too slow
For man's eyes to mark, less
Swift than shells grow.
Inhabitants of darkness,
Dragged up to the light,
Bend their graven faces
Back to night.

Nothing from without
Can break their calm.
—The warm snout of a rock
Nuzzles my palm.

Full in the Late Beam—

Full in the late beam pouring through the cloud-slit,
Pine, hemlock, birch, chokecherry by the road
Dipping and climbing, stand on hills, in hollows,
Singly, in crowds; indifferent to me,
Self-sunk, deep-living, charged; aloof, not hostile;
If I can come through to them, well and good,—
The wall between us is worn thin as paper
(Though tough as horn for all its show of thinness).

I am astonished at the tumult in me.
On this strange road I for the first time travel,
It is as though I came on reminiscence
Not easy to unravel; left and right
I take on my cheek the light-hand touches of love.
Solicitings forgotten, secret, shut
Like nuts in burrs, riddles long buried under,
Pester again, old unremembered seeings
That made the blood flog in its narrow channels
On nights of fall or afternoons of winter
Besieging under cover of this new.

But half this tumult is new-minted loving
Of the new thing itself. See how this hill-side
In a trice becomes familiar-new, nigh-old
On the instant of seeing, through an embrace of the spirit.
All life's enforced habitual withstandings
Against solicitation of the sense
Give way before this utter worth, this sought-for
And found at last off-hand, like a pebble, a feather.

Under a sky like this, in air like this,
Where color and shadow strike down through the turf
Grave-deep, I turn to earth with affirmation.
The open head of the hill banded with shadow
Is a knocked bell, the green-gold field of stubble

Kindles right inward; I am near believing
That, all one impact-spark, the flashing rock-pile
Across the valley in the clearing owns
My seeing eye and signals me with fire.

Moon-Rise

Seeing the great moon rising
On the edge of night,
Over quiet country
Shedding light;

Seeing the full moon rising
Haloed and slow,
Over darkened country
Shedding glow;

In silence, and shadow
Tongued and long,
I hear my heart smitten
Sound like a gong:

"Solitary!" "Endless!"
"Transitory!"
"Flood-swept!"—Thus my heart
To the moon's glory.

I see the moon in heaven
Like an orange haw;
I see the lighted lamp
That Shelley saw.

Small things in the grass pipe
At that amazing glare,
And Awe and Wonder, feathered,
Pass me on air.

A Scant Year

O hand-high raspberry bush
On the rock's shoulder,
Yellowing out of reach,
Your labors done
Before fields bleach
Or seeds down-scatter:
O hand-high raspberry bush
In a cobweb tatter,
Up the steep boulder,
On the rock's roof
In the fierce sun,
Dust on your head, and rust,—
In drouth you have done more
Than I—I see the proof:
One berry, and one core.

Country Miracle

As I came over the rise by Stewart's ash
In the evening early, and caught sight of home,
I stopped two fields off, seeing what I saw:
The Hustons and the Cosmos in such bright
Concatenation as had never been,
Ten odds to one, since first there was a Huston.

In the empty sky above the open hill
A cockle-shell of cloud the length of the roof
(No other in the whole sky anywhere)
Hung low above the old bright lamp-lit house
That rayed out yellow light from every window.
It was the kind of cloud angels would crowd on
In an old painting—Giotto knew the kind—
More raft than cloud; it barely cleared the chimney,
Cusped with a crescent moon, pranked with a planet.

Incredible juxtaposition, stylized, fleeting!
I never saw so pointed a fable, so narrowed
A doing of nature's, as that night I saw
(So pointed a fable, with so hid a meaning):
Forefather's roof, cloud, moon, and Jupiter
Whirled in together for a moment of time
In the enormous scheme, to whirl apart forever.

—Why single out the Hustons, why stoop down
Thus to their hill-head, take their roof for a measure?
If chance had done this thing, then chance was greater
Than I had any idea of, more to be feared.
Not that it happened on the billionth cast,
But that I saw it, made the miracle;
Whether a hall-mark of authentication
(And seals are made of elements as simple,
Earning significance from neighborhood),

Or a wild throw of the dice that turned up doubles
Before my startled eyes, one thing was certain:
No Woodward, Jones or Baker could have seen
What I saw plain. It was a sight for Hustons.

Pulled in by taut wires—man, moon, cloud, and planet
(Man the last comer by the tick of a heart-beat)—
We met, blind allies punctual to the minute,
As I came over the rise by Stewart's ash.

The Poet

He carries deathlessness about his person
As others carry money, left and right
Conferring it, on a woman, on a weed.
—Take this sea-lavender in the pebble-swale
Where the tongue of the sea can lick it, with a blur
Of blue about it, due to die by winter:
Let but the right eye see it, the right shadow
Fall dark upon it, and it will not die;
It is the man who will die before the weed
And be forgotten; after he is dead,
Men will remember that weed in his stead.

The Meadow Under Vapor

The moon looked in so boldly in the night
I rose to shut its loved face out; and saw
The meadow under vapor. In the moon
Gauze, single-ply, without a break or flaw,

Flowed down the open, took the road's mock-hurdle,
And poured down fields past pine-woods toward the sea.
The chill it sent up moonwards made me shiver.
—That fine-spun fog, unhurried and most free,

What was it doing, with its wily wreathings,
Its coilings, its slow shiftings, its retreats?
Under its specious thinness what was stirring?
Something, or nothing?—Seeing mist in pleats,

I knew then that there hides more under cover
Always than men get word of; that the laws
That blot out tussocks likewise blot out knowing;
That thought's a vapor shuts off sight with gauze.

To E. D. in July

Emily, lie you below
And I above, this morning,
While this same earth you used to know
Stabs deep and gives no warning?
It passes me how it can be
That I instead am seeing
Light loved by you implicitly,
While you resign your being.

Tell me truth, did you find heaven
And your old neighbor, God?
Or is it nothingness, not even
A sleep, beneath the sod?
Did your relentless wish create
What is from what could be;
Or found you one grim predicate
Wherewith nouns must agree?

Listen: the tide is out again;
The rock-weed lies out hissing.
I could weep in the world of men
To think what you are missing.
To your low ear I bring in news
Gathered this same day, giving
A pocketful from which to choose
Fresh from the land of living.

The sun finds garnets on this ledge
The tide's bare hand is slapping;
And where the grass fails at the edge
A poplar bush stands clapping.
Woodpecker drums his hollow log,
Pond-lilies open slow,

Shell-pink upon the cranberry bog
Has just begun to show.

This morning early, Emily,
I saw a crane go wading
About the glassed cove to the knee,
The ripples round him braiding;
The cove out of the mist pulled free
As radiant as a bride,
But smokiness blew in from sea
With the turning of the tide.

Know kittens still lap creamy milk,
Know mice still gnaw the rind,
And like great lengths of waving silk
Hay-fields blow out behind;
Barn-swallows scissor down and up
With tea-stained vests (you know!),
And hawkweed crowds on buttercup,
And elderberries blow.

—Here, take them, Emily, they hurt
In telling; can you bear
To hear of elderberries, skirt
The coasts of sun and air?
Know all that hurt you once hurts still.
Need any tell you how
Night brings the moon, dawn finds the hill?
Want you such hurting now?

Out of the Wave

Under the wave the minnow
Oars unwinking past;
I am a menace to him
That darkens over water.
Let me but lift a finger,
He flees: a gull, a man,
Is shadow with a shape;
One swift, one slow; to be feared.

Yet out of the wave came we,
Out of the quiet place
Where minnows tunnel still
In a world all water.
Through that glass door stepped I;
It latched; but for a sign
I in this body carry
The rhythm of the moon.

The Cut-over Field

With none to balk me, head me off, I broke the smouldering
  oak-branch.
All alone I crossed to touch the singe on the sassafras leaf.
The apple-tree, down heavy hung, buttonholed me, going,
And yarrow, come to bloom again on the edge of the road.

I found a path through bushes and followed it over the bank;
It led to a small three-cornered field on a rise hemmed in with
  fir.
They must have cut it early, for already, low and all over,
Small wild asters covered it, lifting and tossing like froth
In a ground-wind from down under. In flimsy agitation,
Eye-lashed and chilly-colored, they wantoned in the clearing,
Looking by rights an April growth, with winter on the way.

Appropriating left and right, I stood still at the path's end.
I had come on more than I bargained for; the sense was all
  about me
Of myriad lovely goings-on covered up from eyes
In that side-field before night-fall. At the chill turn of the
  year,
In a field I had not known of till it was mine forever,
I was caught up for a moment with the tarnishing bush and
  tree:
"Now I am it, and it is I, speculation withers.
I hide in pure transparency, like water in a glass.
Perceived all ways, known through and through, by heart and
  brain together,
This field goes with me the whole way on an in-leading road."

When I came home, you met me in the darkened door-yard
With what but a gentian in your hand, furled, the last of the
  fall:
You gave me that proved-secret thing, not knowing I had this
  other;
I took it into the house with me; and so I had two.

The Unconsumed

I stand abashed before it,
Made a laughing-stock
By the bloomed-out columbine
Wine-kindled on the rock,

Green on the way to claret
Through smoky purple going,
With one bright leaf burned fully down
Like a by-bloom showing.

Whatever fiery knowledge
Scorches it like this
You might think could not help me much
Who know not what it is;

Yet so keen is the sense
This wiry spread of leaf
Gives me of passion deep-sustained,
I find on this rock-reef

Respite from flagging days
Often: blown coal it is,
Fighting flame-burst; only drouth
Banks back fire like this.

The Mineral Collection

I always knew the Ural Mountains glowed
And burned inside with emeralds and gold,
Copper in clefts, and platinum in rifts
Like tamped-in tin-foil; now my eyes have seen
Splinters from that great beam that braces Asia.
Here in the dark, awake, I see again
Rock out of Mexico, Siam, Peru,
Thrace, Arizona, and the Isle of Malta;
Rock out of Chile burning fiercely, furred
With copper-blue like a king-fisher's feather;
Rock out of Greece, imperishable blue,
Cool blue of the Argives lined with green of the sea;
Delicate rock of India, lightly dyed
With milky azure, peach and apricot;
Rock out of Maine, the ice-like tourmaline
In shattered spars, pencils of frigid rose
And chill black-green, of waters most dilute.
—All these the bright credentials of dark workings,
Compulsions, interminglings, strangest love,
Knittings and couplings known but to the atom.
The thought of those bright fragments wrenched from dark-
    ness,
Of cinnebar and slabs of malachite
And crusts of amethyst, dazzles me still
And raises me on my elbow in the dark.
Recalling topaz split and opal fractured
I tingle: great is life retired in stone;
Great is that obstinate impulsion launched
Against the opposition of the dust,
—Whereof are we; we, and the red-cup moss,
The blowing tree, the boulder, and the fly
In amber under water; quick and slow
Braided in one; one indeterminate life
Riddling the dust. Show me one mote inert.

Learning Letters

Knowing not death comes at prime,
Child, like otter or like bear,
Takes things singly, having time;
Sweet is here, and bitter there.

Tasting deeply, savoring slow,
Such a child I used to be;
Watched the weaving of the snow
Thin against the cedar-tree.

While the white flakes, dark from under,
Dropped a slow net over me,
I stood staring up in wonder,
Seeing whiteness darkness be,

And change changeless.—Double newness,
Utter firstness, untrod shore!
Whiteness dark, unfailing fewness,
I had never seen before.

Her great book become a primer,
Nature, with an arm round me,
Pointed out—I saw them glimmer—
Her first letters, A and B.

Ash

The head of last year's thistle where it lies
On the turf is a silver burr, immaculate;
Bleached out to silver is the pasture wood-pile,
The stake at either end, the tongue of the cart.
To silver in the long run apple-trees
Must come, for all their writhings under bark;
In time, the farm-house roof; the farmer's head;
The farm-house rafters; last, the farmer's bones.

—Fierce cleanness, scouring off all taint of color
We know things by, excoriating softness,
Burning them out like clay crocks in a furnace.
I ache to know what shall be built at last
When this implacable milling shall be done,
Body and spirit in invisible fires
Burned down to ashes—to what end? what end?

These five impervious senses hem us in:
Earth, air, fire, water,—these are what they know,
Dull toward all else; dull as the limpet is
Toward Dante or the spiral nebulae,
And for the self-same reason. Even so
I too, a limpet in a world impinging,
Rocked by immeasurable rhythms of a sea
Pulled and released by an improbable moon—
Moon of a planet of a myth-like sun—
Await new powers of knowing, more intense,
Five senses added to the five I have
If need be, till at last I come on knowledge.

The change-defying: somewhere it stands builded,
Builded of ash fire has essayed to eat,
Builded for ends that only ash can serve;
Ash under flame enduring; inmost, last,
The irreducible ash; the Thing That Is.

The Flying Hill

(From a Moving Car)

Sun crowned one swift-emergent hill
Behind dark others, day being done;
Whereat high, low, dark, bright, slow, swift,
Quick, dead, resolved to one,

Brought to a head, in full accord.
Better than others, somehow best
Unalterably, by time adorned,
Under the topless west

Wheeling and veering, lent, withdrawn,
Gold-turfed, black-burred with pine on stone,
Bright-solemn as an honest thought,
The hill ran by and shone.

—Then did approximation die.
I heard, if for a moment's space,
Not assonance's half-way chime,
But the full peal of rhyme!

Meadow's Edge

I was spawned by the earth. It bore me.
I have blind ways of knowing. I trust them.
The flame-girdled meadow in autumn
Does for me more than I know of.

On the edge of the meadow when frost comes,
When waist-high is flattened to knee-high
And whitened with blowing, one glitter
Like water without any wetness;
When frost puts a match to the fringe-growth;
—What with the sharpness, the brightness,
What with the newness, the stillness,
I own the umbilical tie
Like a child on the knees new-delivered.

Jones's Pasture

Now is earth visibly gone over to spirit.
Bushes are more than bushes in this light.
Low sun, rolled cloud, and mile-long shadows cast,
Wild freshness, sharpened air, bathed sight, bare being,
Invade this old and all but empty pasture.

Seeing this ground under on-coming night,
Lit by the colored sun down-rolling, dusk
Behind each reddened bush (and more than dusk),
I am back at the beginning, out of dust, in dew.
This, this is dawn, this is primeval dew,
Death all to be, man unbegotten, life
Dazzling fire-naked over the face of the earth,
Licking up dust like stubble, without smoke.

Toward Speech

A red scarce-opened lily looked me in the face
When I climbed across the stone-wall. Rain was in the cloud,
And a sighing in the birches; and all the rising ground
Across the bay lay sobered, as if to speak truth out.

A tall red twin field-lily in a place unlikely stood,
Knowing I must cry out when I saw it by the thorn;
As wind bent down the bushes, it leaned upon that arm
Lightly, and swayed a little, that morning before storm.

The pine-top by the inlet was a black brush on the sky;
Indigo shook in the distance; and still unaltered came
The dark speech out of scrub and the dark speech out of stone;
But the bright out-breaking lily was one syllable said plain.

Thunder-Tempest

Before the black front of this storm
Man, backing slow, retires
Craving forgiveness.—On it comes,
Leaving a wake of fires.

Thunder topples left and right,
And lightning cracks the sky,
Standing on end to brandish long
In the blinded eye.

Darkness of doomsday shutting down
Like grave-earth on a mouth;
Terror of darkness all about,
And copper in the south;

Rain spouting, wind torn loose, black fringe
Down-trailing from the cloud,
The barn's great peak defenceless,
The roof above us bowed,

Surviving momently we live
Amid the bolts unspent.
—Death is but death: we throw ourselves
Upon the element.

Apostate

Once in a half-light under pine
I saw—and thought I saw amiss—
What was by rights a tree, made vine,
Surrendering upright for supine.
What root-betrayal had done this
I could no more pretend to say
Than why night is not ever day.
Wild apple, abject, shunned the light
As if it knew what it had done,
And was as glad to be out of sight,
Away from eyes and the stare of the sun.

I saw betrayal at the root
Of a wild tree off-hand debase
A stiff-pronged carrier of fruit
Into a vine for a rock's face;
Saw dark incitement lodged in deep
Able to make what's upright creep,
Cancel direction, of itself
Toss time's hard earnings on the shelf,
Cross nature, and with one mad fling
Turn up this flat apostate thing.

The Crimson Point

The short precipitous point is matted over
With a fierce thatch of huckleberry crimson,
Up through which birch-beginnings jet a spray
Of gold-bright drops that hang and do not fall;
The pines are wedged with shadow, and the water
At the point's foot might be from an indigo-pot.
Deep-sunned, deep-shadowed, final every way
(Ice in the air under the beat of the sun)
—This is what I find, looking across the cove
Under my hand this morning after frost.

The edge, the definition, of this seeing,—
The shadow of the chimney on the roof,
The shadow of the boulder on the ledge,
The shadow of the grass-blade on my foot,—
Startles me like the patness of an answer.

But more than sharpened edges are at work here.
The point is sure of something and affirms it
On color's oath, never to be rescinded.
Sheer certainty beats down across the cove
Like sun upon a wall; I warm myself
In its blaze, though harboring darkness at the centre.

Finding this whole too charged for any handling,
Too much of a lightning-bolt to grasp and live,
I say (remembering how a bundle is broken
A stick at a time),—"I will begin with color."
But color too is a bundle.—"Start with crimson."
One at a time, I wrestle with top-colors
And cannot throw them,—yellow, crimson, blue,
Blue, crimson, yellow, proofed like Jacob's angel.
—"Try sound, then. Break it down to speech. Subdue it."
The point gives out a shout; I hear the sound,
But nothing that's a word.

Sitting in flesh,
Which I make to brush aside like a film from my eyes,
I know I am confronting consummation.
—O bright configuration of this shore,
Can you be outwardness? Hear me deny it
With all my members. This is inwardness
Past all I know: it storms the very centre.

In Conclusion

If I could live year-round upon this hill
I should be wiser, but I could not prove
Even then some things I know.—Say what you will,
The sweet-fern leans against the log for love.

Beyond the reach of argument with me
Is the purple on the shingles of the shed
That kindles as the sun sinks. When I see
Mist fill the lowlands as I go to bed,

I know I am through with cleverness, I know
That earth's great pulse ignores it; though it run,
It cannot overtake that logic slow,
Uncontroverted, making nine fields one.

The Dark-Blue Morning-Glory

I know now how the dark-blue morning-glory
Feels in its velvet first-hour, motionless
Pulled sunwards; so the top stands up on its toe
In one place, steady, and the humming-bird
Makes a taut mooring off the larkspur spike.

I may be wrong, I may be wrong, but surely
These blue too-quiet flowers are whirlpool-centred:
—As who can doubt, seeing how on either hand,
Centre-engrossed against disintegration,
The sum of things subsists? Hung on the night,
With slumber at the core, like dynamos,
The atom prospers, and the galaxy
Stands up in arms against the Great Dispersal.
And shall the flower go free, the perishing flower?

The top of motion wears the look of rest—
This much I know; but do the words read backward?
Is rest but top-speed? Almost I believe it.
Seeing this blue hushed vineful tugged one way
Wearing its secret and ulterior look,
I am admonished stillest is most active.

Caught in the drag of the intake, spun to a centre,
No eddies torn from eddies in me left,
No deep divisions, multiplicities,—
Dawn into one, as single as a flower,
I stand at rest on the spiraling Vine, full-blown.

II

To a Forgotten Dutch Painter

The wheat-straw hangs down broken; the nicked leaf
Deploys on air; the snails drag shells like trinkets;
And Master Fly sits in his spot of sun
Upon the yellowing leaf.—This tells me all.

You are a poet, for you love the thing
Itself. In twenty ways you make me know
You dote on difference little as that which sets
Berry apart from berry in the handful.
—"How singular is nigh-identical!"
You cry to dullards; given eyes, we see
The split pod or the briared vine house contraries
Narrowly opposite in a tent of sameness
(Not one but has its urgency upon it).
—"In deep, at the pith, where life makes push, it sits,
The I, the me, the myself, of the cherry,"
You say so plain that I can never doubt it;
—"Sit down before a clover-head," you say,
"As if it were a city to be taken.
Invest it round. There is but little hope."
—"The poppy-seed is a commodious place,"
You urge, and prove it; I behold for you
The negligible ort assume its state
And bridle like a girl looked on with love.

Though all must be whelmed under, yet on the brink
These keep a slippery foothold for a while;
Safe still your darling seed-wafts, drupes and umbels.
Your purpling gooseberry hung by a hair
Has faced down doom; doom looked twice, and went by. . . .
The thing loved well carries the mark upon it.
It outbeams radium. And time lets it be.

Bright Traverse

(An ant runs down a page of Keats in the sun)

I

Down this amazing floor, too flat, too bright,
To be a leaf by oak or maple shed,
Or moose-wood, after frost has cut the thread,
The ant runs circling, maddened by sheer white:
—*"Do trees shed leaves like this?"* (Would God they might!)
"A pest upon this dazzle overspread
With sooty trackings! Give me back instead
The dark I know, my run-way out of sight."

From nought to being, driven by secret rage,
We run out headlong:—*"What's this underfoot,*
This blinding sun-strip, this appalling leaf
With dubious markings?" For a moment brief,
Down deathless words, to him a sprinkle of soot,
So runs the ant across John Keats's page.

II

Are we by this much better off than he,—
That we surmise ours is no common fall
Of soot? Too even-spread it lies, and all
Run straight across with narrow lanes, we see,
As if a giant rake had purposely
Combed the thin dust; and seeing, we recall
(Pattern identical but scaled down small)
The look of a printed page: may it be? may it be?

Order at least; this alms tossed to our want.
Farewell then chaos; that long reign is done.
Farewell the panic of the purblind ant.
Order: a blunt wedge, but our only one,
Good for coarse work. No wedge of man's make yet
Has spread locked lines, pried out the alphabet.

No Myth

(After Winchester)

It is no myth, then. An unresting wheel
Indeed bears down our shrilling generation,
Incredulous that it can lose its station,
And sink from sight, and lie beneath a seal.

Like a rammed thorn it comes, like an angry burr
That sticks in the mind and stings it.
                                        —I have seen
Across a sudden abyss, no plank between,
Canute's bones hoarded up in Winchester.

Main Roads

Few at the most are true kinds. Merging fast,
Like by-ways into high-ways all things flow;
And on the fingers of one hand at last
We may tell off the sum of all we know.
The sudden thought that beckons we see wind
Devious but sure back to some charted track
Worn broad and smooth by pacings of man's mind
In its long goings-out and comings-back.

These are the channels into which my thought
Runs without trying, like water into sluices:—
The sense of life in the earth; truth, candle-sought;
Wonder at beauty; the sweet and bitter uses
Of love; the shortness of man's time on earth,
Its taste like honey, and its utter worth.

Country Neighbor

"Good-bye dear, I'll hope to see you next year
If we're all here," she said from the door-step, frail
As milkweed down, or dandelion, or thistle.
Her white hair showed how yellow-white it was
Against the bone-gray door. I knew she had
As much chance as the dandelion-seed
Lodged under the edge of the shingle had, to cheat
The wind all winter and be there in the spring;
As much chance as the thistle-blow that hung
In the cobweb by the window,—and no more.

The run-out blue-bells growing on a slant
Beside the bulkhead bowed in the wind from the sea
That raked the door-yard, till the plantain leaves,
Blown up from behind, stood white about the woodpile;
The corners of the barn in every shingle
Sang, and the apple-tree was full of minor.
The reek of the barn-yard struck in like a blow
Stinging with life.—("*Men pass but here am I
Spawning new life.*")—"Good-bye." The wind grew shrill.
He tucked her in. She waved her sprig of tansy.

In Token Whereof—

A cottager in Scotland, I have read,
Who in old days bought plough-land, from the spot
Bore home a sod cut from the middle plot,
As proof past doubt, plain even to his poor head.
If he at night bewildered in his bed
Awoke, his hand quick reassurance got
By finding within reach the nub it sought:
"No dream; the field is mine; I shall have bread."

Child, he, or wise man, leaning thus on his
One turf? Both, say I. Thumb-push may not lie.
I too might doubt now,—had I not this clod
Of verse torn from it living (feel of this!)—
That my two feet once trod on floorless sky.
A dream, no more? *What make you of this sod?*

The Passing of the Hay-Barn

When we reached the bend of the road and came on the roar
And the small crackle under, we stopped short in our tracks.
The roof had fallen in; the frame stood up
A blazing crate of timbers still untilted,
Flagged all along with tatters of flame blown sideways.

The old white-chimneyed house under the elms
Stood in the glare unharmed. The morning-star
Was fabulous. Out of the darkened west,
Low, reddened to its setting, the full moon
Looked in like a great melancholy eye.
The dead of night was round; meadows below
Gave up their chill; dew wetted down the stubble.
No breath of wind was stirring, no sound but the fire's.

The little crowd of neighbors stood round watching
The bright malignant thing that reared its head
Thus without warning in their silent fields.
That brash display and flicker of fangs the land
Repudiated; turned its back; and slept.
The fields had other business at that hour
Of night; relinquished small concerns to men . . .
There was nothing to do but let it burn out.

That night I hardly slept for having caught
A glimpse of the universe under a north light.
Hay-barn or planet—does it signify?
An ancient inmost frame gone down the wind,
Become a puff of smoke; given back; at one . . .
Seeing the frame of anything consume
Is solemn business when you come full on it:
Annihilation getting in its work
At top-speed, unmasked, is no sight for children.

All night under sleep I bore the brand of a grid-shape
Far-gone. Saw girders consuming. Not of a barn.

Not Bronze

When I saw the singing word-shape bright and rounded
And hollowed like a bell,
I could not wait to find out how it sounded
In that rich cell.

And so I struck it,—shamed it, made it stammer,
Forced it to tell
With its own tongue, it was beneath the hammer
Not bronze: no bell.

Impaled

(*After Reading Blake*)

Death-rapture is no less catastrophe
That the beheld-perfect has us on its spear-point.
A lost death-fluttered butterfly,
Pinned to the cork at last, run through the heart,
Now as I die, I testify
The instrument of death doth satisfy.

Winter Night

See how the two halves of this shawl opposed stand out on air,
Pushing apart, come all alive; see how this tissue scarf
Runs out to meet and cling to them. Here in this lamp-lit room
I stand dismayed at atom-pranks, my feet upon a brink.

Stranger am I to my shawl, stranger to my scarf.
They raise a shout to elements out in the nebulae.
Beneath my eyes they do a rite, they crackle, spit, and hiss,
Repudiate me, run me through, sting me with knuckle-sparks,

—Till "Yes", I own, and "True", I own, "I am indeed a fool
Who ever thought you were dead things my hands could lay
    away,
While all the time, cried you but 'Hist!', in from between the
    stars
You might have called confederates to end me where I stood."

When I Consider

When I consider all undying hungers
That cut both day and night
Like broken glass, or birds' claws, scratching, scratching,
Forever busy with us out of sight;

When I find all these hungers unavailing,
And in my hands this crust,
My feet upon a road without returning,
My body crying on its way to dust;

When I remember how the years go reeling
Like silk from off a loom,
—Life then, a panther lashing, in me crouches
To spring, but finds no room.

Well Met

You are one of the few who matter, of those whom I count
On the fingers of one hand. I marvel we live
Together in time. When I think how easy it is
To miss one man in the jungle of time, I quake.
Thinking of those long-dead and of those unborn,
Sprinkled apart like stars in the dark, I cry,—
"Whoever else has been missed in the dark—the true,
The bright, the deep-to-be-loved—it has not been you!"

Wing-Spread

The midge spins out to safety
Through the spider's rope;
But the moth, less lucky,
Has to grope.

Mired in glue-like cable
See him foundered swing
By the gap he opened
With his wing,

Dusty web enlacing
All that blue and beryl.
In a netted universe
Wing-spread is peril.

Seeing the Trees Bud

This too in me is life of a kind, this hunger
Unmet forever, driving me down before it.
"Empty!" I cry. And I beat on fences as rigid
As cliffs on a mountain. Not they, but I, shall be broken.
Yet so for a little, it happens, yet so for a little,
I know that I live on this ball of the earth, that I draw
Air into my lungs like a knife: that not yet I die.

Respite

Life caught me up and cast me on your breast
For a moment only, as a wave of the sea
Flings up a drowning man upon a coast.
That gasp of sweet air is his peak of life;
The lift of land beneath, his top of joy;
And though his ears already catch the roar
Of the green on-racing inescapable wave
That comes to drown him, he lies never caring.

Quatrains

Here is the pillow for my weary head;
Here is the great rock-shadow in a land
Of blazing noon where springing shoots fall dead:
Art is. The implications thereof stand.

I must admit the witness of my sense,
I must bow to the clamor in my blood:
Somewhere abundance is, though far, far hence;
Somewhere, beyond this back-wash, there is flood.

Nothing can help. There are no substitutes.
Sometimes I say there are so I can live.
But I know better. Only food can feed;
Not air, not dust, not water through a sieve.

You draw me up to a peak as the moon's long fingers
Pull up the slack of the tide. From least to most,
Heaped on myself, I rise, a hill of water
That leaves a naked coast.

A Modern Psalm

Your oyster is your true philosopher,
Who makes the impenitent sand-grain in his vitals
The bed-rock of his pearl; when he is done,
Inclusion so complete becomes exclusion.
"—What's this you say about a grain of grit?
I have no such about me. You mistake."
Nor could another find the hated speck,
Deep now within the pearl.

                                    Selah.   Amen.

Free Gold

You are a mine to dig in. Long ago
I found a piece of drift so peppered with gold
In pin-points that I could not rest until
I found the lode it came from. It was you.
I sold my house, I sold my land. I came.
There is but little free gold in this world.

Down, down, through foliated strata, down
Through rubble and shale and granite dykes that run
Where once were cracks that led from central fire,
I dig for quartz, dig in the dark for white.
Unless I am mistaken utterly,
I should uncover splendor hereabouts;
Unless the great vein on the surface runs
To nothing in the dark, I soon should see
By the light of my lantern a great glare of white,
And milky quartz should open to my pick,
Quartz full of yellow nail-heads sown in thick.

Antiphony

"The thought of you is sweet to me
As a patch of bayberry
On an island in the sea."

"—*The thought of you is sweeter far*
Than the pinched wild roses are,
Blowing on the harbor bar."

"—Sweet as bayberry the tide
All but comes at, lunging wide
At its russet under-side."

"—*Sweet as roses pink with salt,*
Running headlong down a fault
Till the pebble-swale cries halt."

"Oh sweet as rose"—"*As bayberry*
On the salt floor of the sea"—
"The thought of you to me!"—"*To me!*"

Pause

I wait upon the ledge, deeply and quietly living;
In the hush before the rain I pause and live to the root;
What I know now is more than the sum of what I can see and
   handle,
I am laid open to living, made without warning acute.

This dropping down of a curtain, this sliding back of a bar,
Leaving me at life's mercy for the space of an hour or so,
Also leaves me free to grope with my hand for truth,
And know it queerly by touch as a blind man knows the snow.

Bleak Frontiers

These are bleak frontiers. Nothing old is left.
I walk through turning blades. There is light that kills.
Bleak, bleak, the waste of truth—a polar place.
Can anything that lives find foothold here?
Such glacial edges can drive men before them
Till they come to ultimate shingle, facing a void.

Yet even as I face this frigid tract,
I know that time wears down the stubbornest rock
To soil again; it makes of flint a seed-bed
Fit for arbutus or the lady's-slipper.
Substance is friend to life, from everlasting;
Form is the foe, form is the enemy
The living have a right to be afraid of.
And time wears form out. This is so. I grant it.
—Yet now I blench, walking this bladed ice,
Tapping this ringing ledge, looking for life.
Oh for a patch of green the size of a hand;
That somewhere on iron rock I might find live moss!

The Backward Pupil

Before we have learned to live we must learn to die.
These lessons crowd too fast; this Taskmaster
Drives for promotion. I would linger learning.
I like the sound of words like "bell" and "snow"
And "love"; I want to say them over and over.
—"Make haste. You waste your time. We start tomorrow
New words."—"Oh why? Let me take this term's work over.
By slow, by slow, by roundabout and slow,
I yet might come (who knows?) on what is simple."

The End That Awaits

There is a new sound in my ears; a sound where but now there
was silence;
There is a new sound in my ears, more faint than mist over
spray,
Unbodied as vapor at moonrise, or fog dimming a fir-tree.
I know it will not grow less—it is due to mount into thunder.
I know it for what it is: the leap into space of a river.
There is a new sound in my ears. It is the sound of the end.

The end. The end that awaits. The end that may not be evaded.
The cataract known by report, now nearing, come within ear-
shot.
The banks slip no faster away, but sun and green are made
precious.
There is a new sound in my ears: it is the sound of the end.

The Last Stand

"When you shall fail me, on that day
When white for me goes black,
Down drops the wall that holds at bay
The darkness and the pack."

—So once. Now each appalling raid
Breaks on the inmost wall.
I am my own last palisade.
When that falls, I shall fall.

Softly There, Master-Logician

You tell me that water this once has risen above its source;
That life has come from not-life on this lost and wandering
　ball.
You say this, hemmed in a cover from which there is no break-
　ing out,
Shut in a thicket of alder.—Knowledge forgets its foundation
Is airy, a cross-cut of sunbeam. Go softly there, master-
　logician!
Of all the houses we build the sills and cross-beams are
　guesses;
Only the shingles and sheathings are handled and known and
　dependable.
Timbers of poets have lasted longer than those of logicians.
Softly there, master-logician; softly there; humble is best.

Stewart's Ash

                                       —Oh what
Has happened overnight to Stewart's ash
That it stands up stripped like Lear?

It has scissored down its sombre cover like litter,
All of it in a night, and made an end.
Making the last relinquishment of all
As if it were nothing, in the windless dark
(Since frost is frost) it cuts the business short.
No dallying maple inching in retreat
Could do this thing; mark the stiff back-flung gesture
Of the great brush, which well might stand for pride.

Leaf-fall a man can bear; but double-fall
Is destitution; pity one when leaves
Fall in the heart too, simultaneous drop
Unthreaded.—I remember still the day
When Stewart's ash tree failed me. It stood up
Like the end of hope, the gray cross on a grave.
No longer able to bear up the weight
Of meaning I had life-long shelved away
On its great top, it shed it with its leaves;
Striped now of the factitious, a forked stick,
It stood up bare, never to bud again.

—So it seemed then. Yet in its new blank role
It proved a deeper mystery than before.
Deeper but different. So one might feel
Who had come on the skull of his friend, expecting his face.

We have at best but knowledgeable symbols,
That point us this way, that way. Not for nothing
The leaned-on failed me when the new stood ready.
Knowledge comes ache-wise. I am one who knows it.

III

Now Under Summer

Now under summer runs the first ground-swell
Of coming autumn. Bow down, bright adored
Greenness of summer, for your end is toward,
A tide comes on, slow, ineluctable.
Oh who can tell of autumn, who can tell
Of consummation with a wooden word?
Let him declare your face, Jehovah Lord,
Where high between the cherubim you dwell.

There are no words for such, for they unspell
All words and make a heap. When waved the sword
Before the Garden's gate, no sound was heard.
There is no clapper in the gold-bronze bell.
Before such ram's-horn blasts, such trumpet calls,
Words fall down flat like Jericho's quick walls.

What Once I Was

Flesh and blood refuses pain
Such as this. I have been rash.
These old fields seen once again
Ply me with a knouted lash.

Buried deep within the mass
Of these hills that take the glow
Still subsists what once I was,
Shouldering under indigo.

It confronts me, bids me strip.
—Time, like kersey stand between
Naked flesh and flying whip,
What now is, and what has been!

By my own self I am torn
(Most of all I fear that tooth),
Beating off like bundled thorn
Innocencies of my youth.

First Night of Fall

(Hunter's Hill)

Earth might look like this to an angel flying over,
Twice as deep-seen, bright-seen, as our eyes are used to.
Doubtless hills the Flood drenched looked so that first
    summer.
Through the air of crystal, see the end-on cornfield
Twisting up the steep slope like a Roman ribbon,
And the killed fir, singled by the low sun, kindling
At the bottom of the crimson on the eastern shoulder.

Across a field of shadow to a hill of brightness
Looking mortal-eyed for a deathless minute,
Chill rising round me, dahlias marked for dying
In a rank before me, soon to be cut off,
I, till now immortal, know all in a minute
How short the shift of life is, how sharp the knife is whetted.

What's Over

Though heaps of shucked-out yellow corn shine along the
    stubble,
The crow detects a season of scant picking coming on;
Wild aster does not fool itself; though frail like something
    spring-like,
It stands in the sure knowledge spring is past and gone.

But you debate the seasons, and your words are an affliction;
No truth stains them from under as the blackberry's leaves are
    dyed.
—Know then, what's over's over: illiterate denial
Is only hollow shell-ice or life-everlasting dried.

The Day of the Small Bush

The thinned gold tree stands precious. This is the day
Of the small bush unregarded: gold worth descends on weeds.
The burning-time of little tips is over
Up on the side of the mountain, on the shelf, in the seam of the
   ledge.
Already the young quick-frightened poplars have tossed
Their cover of saffron to earth, already the darkened ash
Draws near to its undoing as if it knew it,
And off on the edge of the rise the birch trunks show like flaws
In the rim of the world, like white cracks in blue sky.

Say nothing for a little; bear with me; I have seen
The cherry tree in tatters hanging down,
Fever and pallor there contending for one leaf;
I have seen the maple in the stone-wall, lifting
Its scatter of star-cut leaves paler than any straw-stalk,
Stand up thin-rigged against the ink-blue water
Where the sea's arm makes in at the foot of the tilted pasture.

The lift in the wind, the chill in the air, the scorch of the frost,
Make summer a thing gone over; this is what's left.
—Oh rich fag-end! In a flurry of leaves on the floor of the
   gully,
The tall wild aster lays its chilly plume
Windily to the boulder, bending to recover;
Wind has its organ note of fall; rustling of paper
Moves with me down the field; gold tags, gold patches,
Are caught on the bramble bush; the drawn-out flicker of
   flame
Tied to the twig, here, there, by invisible thread,
Still holds against the wind bent on blowing it out.

The thinned gold tree stands precious. This is the day
Of the small bush frost-discovered; gold worth descends on
   weeds.

Aloud Out of Nothing

"Why act the part of Myself?—Evans as 'Evans'
Cumbers the stage. Forget the part. Be Evans.
Say, 'I have forgotten the cue,'" I found myself saying
Aloud out of nothing, as if a bubble up-gathered
At the bottom had swum to the top, the time being ready.
"Nothing can last that is not in itself
As real as copulation or as death."
At night-fall, under stoked glow and rag-work of leaves
And rick-rack of boughs against sky, I found I knew this.

Thin Ice

Skate out on thin ice, skirt the edge of death,
Of life; pray God to be the weight of a leaf.
No thought now but one flying thought before
To travel with us over buckling ice.
No pause, lest all about we hear the sound
Of crackling glaze, like twigs beneath a pot.
Each rod is so much gain, odds wrung from chance.
Hereafter life for us lies only in speed.
I am become a passionate hope, the stale
At last become sharp salt, now the stake is my life.

Frost Is on the Bunchberry

Cold cannot hurt this country huddled under hemlock;
It ekes out cover of a kind, what with spruce and fir
And threadbare birch and alder. This chill means snow;
But fields are ready for it, they are not caught napping
Though the sun goes wan now, skimmed over like the pools.

Frost is on the boxberry, on the hard-hit bunchberry,
Where Bokhara color darkens half the pasture.
Everywhere I look I see numbed small ones
Wearing bronze and dull maroon, like men enduring time.
Frost is on the matted grass at the edge of the alder-swamp,
And the young juniper, just taking hold,
Side-tilted, new-alighted, with a claw stuck in,
Shivers on the south slope.—How long till snow? How long?

At night the wind complains long in the narrow box
Of the raging airtight stove in the plain room.
Stars glitter round the chimney. How safe the low black barn is
Under the Dipper's handle, arched over like a wing.

The Cup Out of Ur

When I saw the cup out of Ur,
And found it was silver,—
Not zinc the nerveless, not that one,
But silver, the knitted, the rustless;
When I saw what mere thousands of years
Had done to it, how they had leached it,
And left it a mouldering substance
Aged and other, like lead;
When I saw the failure of shape,
The cup fallen in on itself,
The terrible caving from weakness,
From pith of silver gnawed out:
    Then—then only—I knew
    What Time is. I met it. I shook.

Sonnet

I did not guess the hurt had gone so deep
Till it came out the midmost clove of a song,
Giving words life. In at the heart of the heap
I saw, deep-buried, what made those words strong.
I saw which thorn of beauty that made sting
My heart long since, here issued as a flower;
And learned how long in the dark a living thing
Lies unregarded, waiting for its hour.

No blue-flag by a water-hole in summer
Hides in its yellowing pod a thing more sure
Than I this day shut up from the chance comer
In the long dark to greaten and mature.
Strange bees have left me fertile; out of sight
I bear black seed which yet shall come to light.

The Sycamore in Winter

Toy-balls tied to the twigs jerk in the norther.
Not a leaf is left on the rack. Not that it matters.
This honest moving plain asymmetry,
Striking its own law out on the spur of the minute,
Achieves a balance that is more than beauty.

So this is what the tree was coming at
Under all the lovely balderdash of summer
And babble of leaves: the gist of the matter made plain
In these whipped balls, gut-hung against the winter,
Tussling till spring against the wind's to-do,
Till chamois snippets star the ends of branches
And the whole circle is to run all over.

In these small danglers with their dead-in-earnest
I see Creation shouldering its burden.
—To each, in fine, a thing to do: between them
The stars maintain a north; the sun goes trudging
Its widening arc; the raindrop holds together;
The tree, come spring, has brought its business through.

All is as simple as necessity.
As simple and as secret. Under-slung
Travels the baggage of the universe.

Time's Cap-Poem

The terrible whorl of the Milky Way shines out
To newt-eyes under; glory bears down ton-like;
Ordeal girdles us in. I marvel we live.
Yet live we do in the maelstrom, mites as we are;
On our acorn shook from the Oak we ride out the dark.

"The nature of the universe is such"—
(So Einstein, writing thereby time's cap-poem)
—"The nature of the universe is such
A thing may verily be forever unknowable."
Forever unknowable: here is the longest lane
Without a turning, down which we must wander
Lightless forever, being what we are,
Being shut in man-shape, and not rock- or wind-shape
With who knows what organic ways of knowing.

Though God has fallen in this latter year,
Dragging what with him, still given mystery
We can endure, given mystery to draw from.
Cross knowledge off; it does not matter much.
In old sum-total darkness such as this
May lie wrapped up what couples and what counters,
What God-to-be along with old God fallen!

Nothing is sure and all is possible.
—The path that bears off inland yet may bring us
To the edge of a cliff dropped seawards: may; may not.
In place of fear, we have a right to hope;
In a place of hope, we have a right to fear:
Here is a balance never to be broken.
"The nature of the universe is such
A thing may verily be forever unknowable."
—Man, back-retired in man-ship, therein breathes:
Within a diving-bell we live in the sea.

152

Slow Gain

The silky sweetness of a full-blown thistle
Is arrowy, goes in deep,
Turns to felt truth, a latter-day Epistle,
Becomes a Law to keep.

Aprils lived through, Julys and fierce Decembers,
Let down a silt, a dust
Of gold, like brooks.—Truth lodged thus in our members
Is the truth to trust.

Fact of Crystal (1961)

From an Offshore Island

(September Gale)

Hear now the ocean trouncing off this island,
The under-roar of wind down unfenced sea,
And through chance flaws, like dim light down a tunnel,
The bell buoy spent with distance.

Orion's chill, washed, subterranean glitter
Wheels up from under, and great Rigel blazes
Between tossed oak boughs that the gale of autumn
Tears at, lifts, lets fall.

Old ocean's hoarse and implicated roaring
Brings me up sitting at the dead of night,
Its pent-in mouthless fury calling back
The wild first of creation,

The rage, the might, the rampage.
                                              —How shall I
Up from this anchored island not make answer,
I with my bones of rock-dust hardly knitted
And my blood still salt from the sea?

Tree in Night Wind

Against the stress and drive of my own passion
Filling up every cranny of my being,
The surging of the tree outside my window
Makes headway till I have to stop and listen.

                          With one great light
Green-coruscating myriad-chinking heave
After another, and no rest between,
Opening every last leaf out to air,
The tree protests interminably, agrees,
With a thousand delicate quick afterthoughts
Capping each other like ripples on a shore,
Till each leaf has its say, matters, and counts;
The full-voiced crying when the stress is on
Dying out to next to nothing; then to nothing.

Far off a tree less intricately leaved
Makes simple sound, one-voiced. But this outside
My window says a thousand things at once,
With multiple accents on each separate word.

I listen wondering, hearing the deep wind
Say a serious thing in the most allusive way
That ever was or could be, the tipped leaves
Lipping almost together, but not quite,
With overlapping of the syllables.—I hear
The rainy wind in the dark, the lone sound
Seething, the passionate gust subsiding, the spent leaves
Unclapping, hanging down. Then out of the dark,
Many-tongued, I hear the tree talk: it is more like a crying
When passion departs; how sober, light-swept, grave-lovely,
Till brought again to top cry all surging together!

Yet here is no confusion: central-ruled
Divergent plungings, run through with a thread

Of pattern never snapping, cleave the tree
Into a dozen stubborn tusslings, yieldings,
That, balancing, bring the whole top alive.
Caught in the wind this night, the full-leaved boughs,
Tied to the trunk and governed by that tie,
Find and hold a center that can rule
With rhythm all the buffeting and flailing,
Till in the end complex resolves to simple.

Primary

Few originals, but mighty,
Waking in the prime—
Pull and release, light, sound, growth, color—
Broke through space and time.

Who but God could have imagined
Cineraria blue,
Or seen scarlet in not-scarlet,
Underived and new?

He alone could call from darkness
Yellow yet unhinted
Where it lay a dreaming splendor
Of the mind, unminted.

Green was easy, given yellow,
One made out of two.
But these tunneled through pit blackness:
Scarlet; yellow; blue.

Fringed Gentians

In run-out ground in coveys
They startle; here and there
They put blue in italics
Where few stare.

On the bright edge of meadows
When orchises have dried,
Where cranberries streak carmine
They stand beside.

Tight-sheathed, fierce-single, wiry,
Going about to die
They undertake a color
To rock the sky.

"Why, stern, clip blue down foursquare,
Yet fringe it?"—Steady of eye,
New England answers nothing,
Finger-high.

The Striped Earth

I love the striped earth in the early hour
Of morning when birds breast the colored sun.
The stripes run west then, but the hills have power
To wheel them eastward when the day is done.

Day-break and day-end, banded either way,
Wear stripings for a cloak, a pageant sight:
Earth lying new-created, waiting day;
Earth swept with day remembered, waiting night.

Pegmatite

Here am I relentlessly
Cropping out for you to see
In my final nudity.

This is I and I am this,
Stripped of surface fripperies
That have covered up what is.

Pasture green is well enough,
But earth's core is fiercer stuff
Crammed with flashings in the rough.

Take or leave me; but first think
How gem stuff can pack a chink
Till split edges make men blink.

Clearing After Rain

After warm rain, now that the chill is rising
From the meadow down below, see what a scouring
Away of tarnish from the silver-azure
Inverted bell of heaven; and below us,
Time's reel run backward, in a flash behold
Earth smoking from creation, thousand-fissured.

Folds, points, tree islands, lapped in shreds and tatters
Of vapor bearing south, oppose their dogged
And long-determined bulks to what is weightless.
See now direction regiment confusion:
Cloud remnants troop off marshaled; from the wood lot
And the ridge behind it dragging vapors travel
In leaning crowds that press across the meadow,
Knowing where the river is, going to find it.

In the least twirl of a mist thread down the field,
The slant, the leaning, the most slow prostration,
Nothing is left to chance. I have been told it,
And now I see it. Thus does nature do.
The curls of children are her fingerwork,
The continents her homework, and the stars
Her oldest work of all; what look like lapses
No huggermugger, but brief variants
Pulled back into the pattern, given time.
Slow order is her madness, under all
Working her ends out till the heavens fall.

Northern April

Gray, brown and blue:
Bleached field, bronzed firwood, sky
Like a babe's eye.
Long-legged winds like boys
Race down pastures to the sea,
With a clatter of bone-dry boughs
And locust pods jingling at the ends of branches.

Wan, spent, disheveled,
Saying, "—We have come through,
But that is all,"
The land lies quiet for a little
Before making an effort,
Like a man waking from a fever,
Or a woman who has borne a child.

Euroclydon

The east-northeaster pounds the coast tonight,
Thudding and grinding at the knees of islands;
It sets the bell buoys clanging and calls out
The gruff storm warnings up and down the coast.
—So this, none else, was Paul's Euroclydon,
That old tempestuous wind that leaped from Crete,
And heaped the seas up till they broke the ship,
But not the man.—Pull out the Book again:
"When the south wind blew softly—" (O sweet words,
The spring is in them. Hark!)—"we loosed from Crete."

I sit and listen while Euroclydon,
That old storm wind that had a name of its own
Two thousand years before I yet had mine,
Pelts on my pane with blizzard snow like grit,
Shrieks down my chimney, grips my house foursquare,
And pants against my door.

Old tiger, hail!

Newfoundland Harbor

(A Painting by Arthur Davies)

Not accidental are these spiritual shapes
Seen on this rocky shore; flushed with the red
Of cliffs behind them they delay their running
Down air a moment, manlike but not men.
This solitary cove of fishing boats
We know for their indubitable home.
These are the very spirits of the place
Come visible; their bare emergent forms
Abstracted from the cliffs and luminous air
Authenticate our guesses, burn away
Doubt as the sun burns fog off. While we look
We can no longer tell outer from inner;
Place becomes person, person becomes place.

Make affirmation of what thing you know;
This is the utmost man can do for man.
(So pigment cries plainer than words could do.)
Bring attestation in; record your soundings;
Charts are made this way. Inked-in patient findings
Lessen sea terror; jot by jot brought landwards
("Ten fathoms at this spot"—"A floor of reef"—)
Becomes in time a map, a thing for trust.

This man has set down for all eyes to see
One thing he came on in his hour of living,
His own, seen firsthand, flashingly, not ever
To be let slip: constituent of knowing
Most sure of all because most pure, most blinding.
Such knowing comes to be our only wealth,
Whether hard-earned, slow-apprehended, or tossed
In gratis by the casual lightning flash.

"Inhabitants are these"—who now can doubt it?—
"Inhabitants, not conjured visitants
"Of these flushed cliffs, this solitary cove.
"Once seen is known forever: spirit is here
"Treading this harsh shore lightly, being at home."

Always, wherever we look, single is double,
Like the moon's disc, two-faced; always double is single,
Like the moon's great rondure; old identity
Is all there is; it covers like a hand.

The Iceberg Seven-eighths Under

Under the sky at night, stunned by our guesses,
We know incredibly much and incredibly little.
Wrapped in the envelope of gossamer air,
A clinging mote whirled round in a blizzard of stars,
A chaff-cloud of great suns that has not settled,
By the barn's black shoulder where the gibbous moon
Hangs low, no other light making a glimmer
In the dark country, hearing the breathing of cattle—
I do not need that anyone should tell me
Most real goes secret, sunken, nigh-submerged:
   Yet does it dazzle with its least part showing,
   Like the iceberg seven-eighths under.

River Mirror

(Early Morning)

Take away the mirror.
Men are only men.
Why redouble ever
Finals in a glass?

Wind, do one thing for us:
Stoop from upper air,
Do away with doubles—
Singles we can bear.

Rain at Night

Hearing the gentle myriad rain talking in the night,
Comforting the roots of grass and man's heart by turn,
Catching wisdom's tone therein but the words not quite,
I marvel, thinking in the dark how much I have to learn.

My schooling creeps on like a snail: I have learned the ways of
    men
A little, and of women more; I have yet to learn the ways
Of fox and tiger, oak and fern, the eagle and the wren;
And after these, hid ways of stones, stars, seasons, nights and
    days.

Since so much time has gone to learn so little of the whole,
Since so much pain and joy attend a pocketful of truth,
I fear I need in spite of you duration and a soul,
And to withstand life's full assault strength past all strength of
    youth.

Northern Lights Over Sutton

(*To R.L.F.*)

Down over Sutton swung an incredible tassel
Slung from a knot at the zenith, plying and playing
All loose, shorn across at the bottom as a tassel would be
That covered the island; we looked up into live strands.

Force made visible; bodiless force arrayed
In a veil of shifting light that left it naked.
Seen force: not its end-work but its sheer self
At work or at austere play for that part of an hour
After midnight, surprising a few men scattered abroad
In dark country or on the face of the sea—
A chance fraternity only, roused, called abroad
By the accident of living, to be startled awake
By such an inrush from the outer dark
As dwarfed a planet's doings, made provincial
Earth's local splendors, local cataclysms.

Off sideways through the thin veil that trembled unceasing,
Stars shivered to emerald glints above the dark mountains
Ranged as a backdrop might be for a stage set for mortals:
But not for mortals that unbridled shining
Hanging above, that skein untouchable swaying,
Fading and flaring anew.
                              —Yet did we endure it
Brief-granted, until (as if by a gesture to end it)
The huge red prow of the moon pushed up from the sea
Like a holocaust on an island lost on the sky line.

—Already then, O bright head in the dust,
Omen was shaping: like the first chill muted
Echo of a bell, struck once, far off,
Portent hung over your island on that night of time.

Return to Life

The Southwest wind blows in from the sea unceasing,
The brown hawk falls in the field. Once more I live.
Like a hand pulled free from a glove I finger edges,
Ease and expand like a dry sponge drinking water.
Now like a too-tight cord that can untwist
Its tortured length, and spinning round and round
Resign old tension back into the air,
I am escaped from the thumb and finger of life.
Shaken loose like a tassel at last, I hang, I swing;
A breath can whiff me round, this way or that.

While the robin calls with his colored note for rain
And the bright cattle watch me from the pasture,
The cranberry's cold little apples deep in the marsh
Feel good to my hand that goes groping, sun beats on my
    shoulder,
Heat flatters my cheek, pouring up from the floor of the
    meadow.
Seeing the boxberry plums hid under the leaves,
And this year's arbutus plants, crisped, hugging the bank,
And the lady's-slipper leaves, paired, wedged in the mould,
I dally along at my ease, keeping step with the sun.
I make free with myself at last; I see that we are friends.

Arcturus Through a Spyglass

(A Fable for Realists)

There was an ancient spyglass in the corner
Beside the front door, used for generations
To study out a boat upon the river,
Or pick the stage up, off on Prentice Hill.
Upon a night of stars I took it out,
And steadying its length with quiet blood
I turned it on Arcturus. Once; not twice.

Oh terrible the ebbing out of light
That drained the blazing star to the pale penny
There in the glass. I went faint.—"This, Arcturus?
"So swift the leap from that far-flaming sun
To this dim round of dark and glimmering brightness?"
I reeled and put the glass down, not to see
That quenched unearthly distance-wearied light.
Earth shrunk so small I trembled for my footing.
To see a star all points, and the next minute
Confront instead a sullen minor moon
Dredged up from the depths of space to shock the eye
Was enough for one night; for one lifetime even.

But before sleep the truth came clear and simple.
Above the black peak of the barn it narrowed
To a point and found me as light finds an eye:
Sailboats and stages are the kind of thing
To turn a spyglass on; never a star.
A peep-glass fails, pitted against that great one.
Trued to earth miles it falters among light-years,
Brings in a lie, and scares us with half-seeing.
Only the naked eye with its sure guess
—That, or a godlike glass—can see Arcturus.

To a Poet Yet Unborn

Attempt what's perpendicular. Scale what's impossible.
Try the knife edge between two voids; look into both abysses.
Bring back some word of wordlessness if strength enough is in
    you.
Write doggedly of dizzying things; with small implacable digits
Delimit space to fit the brain, that it may bulk and be.

No one but you can help us much. Subdue what blasts. Dare
    do it.
Ride formlessness, word wordlessness. Be not aghast. Be poet.

Welsh Blood

Welshness is tinder stuff.
Genes of the Britons
Kindle the bloodstream:

Sparkings from old tribes
Backed up in the mountains
—Snowdon, Cader Idris—
Against the Romans;
Under Brecon Beacons
Standing off the Saxons;
On the ribs of seacoast
Fighting the Danes;
Watching castles building
To hold them under;
Mouthing the old tongue,
Believing in magic,
Alive with wonder.

—And all the while,
Bards in the halls of chieftains
Up and down the country;
Words wrought on with love
As gold by goldsmiths;
Consonants and vowels
Echoing and chiming,
Form and pattern honored
Down through savage days
By a small fierce people.

Everywhere singing:
Dark-head and red-head
In the folds of mountains
Plucking the harp strings,
Singing together.

Sound more than sight
Sets the Welsh blood leaping,
Sound of words flung skywards, of throng-singing.
Drum-roll names fill the ear from Menai to Glamorgan—
Caernarvon, Plynlimon,
Tal-y-Bont, Carmarthen.
Still on hills, in valleys,
The shibboleth of Wales
Unmasks the alien—
Llyn Llydaw, Dolgelley,
Llanelly, Llangollen;
North, south, east, west,
The old strange sound lives on.

Here my own father
Worked in the coal seam
Out of light of day,
Going in by starlight,
Coming out by starlight,
First, a child of seven.
Last, a man of twenty,
Throwing down the coal pick,
Crossed the ocean,
Found my mother,
Begot me.

These things are my things:
Purple St. David's
Down in its hollow,
Covered with time's waters
Like a pebble in a cup;
Safe in Aberystwyth
Hoarded like crown jewels,

The Book of Taliesin,
The Black Book of Carmarthen.

The strand is braided in
Past all undoing.
Yes I say to Wales,
Yes Wales says to me.

Past Telling Of

"*I know what rapture is.*"—Once, and no more than this.
His roots reached down in the dark, and a living water gave
Suck as long as he lived.—"*I know what rapture is.*"
Past telling of, his own, he took it to the grave.

A silence where words give out is a well on which to draw;
A well with a living spring; it will not go dry.
Chatter is a pool with the bottom near the top.
Silence is a well. You can draw on it till you die.

All Those Hymnings-up to God

All those hymnings-up to God of Bach and César Franck
Cannot have been lost utterly, been arrows that went wide.
Like homing birds loosed from the hand, beating up through
　　land fog,
Have they not circled up above, poised, and found out direction
(The old God gone, the new not yet, but back of all I AM)?

Such cryings-up confound us; I think they are not tangential,
But aimed at a center; I think that the through-road will follow
　　their blaze.
No man has handled God, but these men have come nearest.
I trust them more than the foot rule. Bach may yet have been
　　right.

This Bridgehead Generation

We are too near. In the face of what we see
Silence is better than the sound of words.
Homer himself sang not till Trojan swords
Were long since rust in an old century.

Not till the tumult dies, and under green
Lie all of us, and time has brought to birth
Poets whose frame-dust slumbers deep in earth
Can men make song of what our eyes have seen.

Havoc

Not of whirlwind, not of flame,
Is this havoc which you see;
Devastation stooped and came
Straight from chaos on this tree.

Nothing black or splintered shows,
As when lightning finds an oak;
But one looking on it knows
It has tasted fire and smoke.

Like a live man still he tries
To endure and seem to be;
At the bottom of his eyes
Death is lying stonily.

Deep Down It Dwells

Things come plain in the middle of the night.
Roiled water clears; we see what's at bottom,
The rock silted over, the water-logged tree.
This turns to that before us—ask not how it happens
We come back fledged with power from the great gulf entered.

Old puzzlements resolve themselves as if by some enchant-
ment;
We swim up out of sleep like the diver with his pearl.
As fearless as a drawing made by the sure hand of a child,
Life assumes an outline; we have a hint to go by.

Come to Birth

All lesser reasons for loving die away
Before this one: that you had power to make
Demand on me which I had power to meet;
That you could make demand so deep that I
Could meet it only by an act of birth,
Watching creation like a looker-on,
Myself the thing created out of dust.
Well may I own the power that does this thing.
With shaken breath I fear to look on the face
Of this great-statured self that bowed in the dark.
Decision now out of my hand is torn
And passes to this other at its birth,
And what shall happen I no longer know.

The Wrestling

> "*Who are you, slim-hipped tussler?*"
> —All night in the dark,
> Like Jacob with his angel,
> I wrestle until dawn.
>
> When daybreak comes, it shows me
> Who was the Adversary.
> I know my topmost worth then,
> The touched thew bearing witness.

Ancestor Forgotten

Dull Theriodont, how were you ever able
To import warmth to the reptilian vein,
And make yourself the corridor, the alley,
Down which the dreaming line of mankind came?

There you veered off, making portentous parting,
Forsaking chill blood and the lidless eye,
And left huge Brontosaurus and his fellows
To breed and wallow on, left crocodile,

While you alone, poor cumbrous brute forgotten,
Blindly forswearing nightmare and hell-scream,
Bore on the future in your loins unwitting—
You, Theriodont, the splitter of the stream.

Pebbles from Sister Island

Eight miles off shore,
Worn down to velvet by the thumb and finger
Of the sea incessant-shaping, tight-grained, polished,
Foreign to granite (these are granite's grinders),
Powdered with salt they lie up. The steep beach
Is strange with jasper and outlandish stone
Dim-colored, brown-flecked, olive, chiefly black,
Most like old pagan basalt from the depths
Bared when the moon tore free.

The night Columbus talked with Isabella
These rocks were slatting on the coast of Maine.
When Rome fell, and Atlantis, they were here.
They rode the glacier down from Canada,
Maybe, in state; and dropped in the sack of the sea.
To-fro, to-fro, interminably washing,
Hurled and haled back with screeching from the shore,
To-fro, to-fro, they carved the great pink-granite
Platform of the island into hollows
Till it stands up from the glass floor of the sea
Like something out of Dali.

On the foot rule of time scaled to the vast they are new,
But their newness is nothing to mine; I tremble before
Their hoary generation. None the less
Let me hold them in my hand a moment, sense
Duration, through delight of touch approve
The buffing of the lapidary sea,
Darkly partake of the being of first rock.

On the Curve-Edge

From the thick cover of unknowingness
Breaking a little farther than the beasts,
We children of the formless, slow to wake,
From that serene circumference delivered
To gale and tumult and the razor's edge,
Cast up and wincing, pick our way down shingle:

On the curve-edge of oblivion to live,
In the shadow of extinction, like the last
Fierce spark that burns on the black rim of the sun
Before the eclipse sweeps over; in the shade
Of a mounting threat to snatch our crumb of joy.

Do we then well to live? Yes, we do well.
Doom halts to topple, but we living lie
Awake in the dark, under terror rich in the peace
Of having drawn breath for this little, knowing we are,
Relishing life, sucking the honeycomb.

Sunup in March

No wonder the birds make whittlings of sound, that the
  hemlock
Prepares to dip and plume in the wind, dead sure
Of what is now on the way from the edge of the world.

That blazing bale in the thicket is bright day
Upbundled, fubbed in a ball: conglomerate glory
Inrolled, constricted to one nub of fire.
See how a whole day rages, telescoped
On itself, foreshortened, to a furnace blaze
Behind the wattle of the alder swamp.
—Or has earth's floor turned into sky's sea bottom
Harboring treasure undredged, a crown-jewel heap
That pooling time's splendor and glitter unwavering burns?

What underbrush can hide a thing like day,
Or hope to hold it with so frail a lattice?
Yet in a snare as it were the great bird of day
Nests for a moment of time on the floor of the swamp.
Presently rising over the rim of the world
It will be on us unmasked; but now for a little
The creature's eye looks level into day's
And sees time end on, burning.

                                      —If a day
Can blind like this, what of a year? Oh what
Of a century at one glance? What of that fury?

By the Salt Margin

By the salt margin where life first broke cover,
The reek of seaweed bids the blood remember.
Struck through with sun, incorporate with ledge,
Like a pelt stretched on a door for the sun to cure,
I now attest existence. Heat pours down
Like rain upon me, drenching the lichened ledge,
The chained-down limpet and the forspent body.

Now side and hand and foot sole have to do
The thinking for me. Tell me not "about,"
Deliver the thing itself, its sting or nothing.
O unworn senses, mint the minutes sharp,
Make each one be a gold piece. Being is all.
I know at last firsthand, as Moses did,
Jehovah's final name is deep I AM.

Fact of Crystal

Who shall say that the rock feels not at all
In its obscure, slumbrous, geologic way
The pinprick of incipient demolition;
Or sensed not once the dream-faint, unremitting,
Electric stir of the crystal rising in its side—
The next-to-nothing gnat-sting, the dim prickle
Of flowering not-life making try at growth,
Prefiguring afar the flying fire
That runs in the veins of men, through coils of time
Bringing prodigious newness out of earth?

Motion, that far-off whisper—it was there
In quartz, in beryl, in the mica sheath.
In crystal-building and in fusion flash
The poles of speed declare themselves, and what
Is cataclysmic, loosed in a splintered second,
Innocuous creeps down its millionth year.

Locked in dragging ages black as Tophet,
Crammed into corners in split seams of the earth,
Down deep in torpor's dungeon lodged forgotten.
Accepting off-slant cramping of the facets
As incidental and of no importance,
These mounting shapes from formlessness arriving
Were not unmindful of their glorious axes
In at the center fixed, ordaining true
The ancient inmost pivots of pure selfhood.

Behold the beauteous sluggards and their work—
The slothful quartz, the lazing tourmaline,
And their great tardy dazzle. Envy rock's glory.
This that hung once thinner than breath in space,
Wraith of a wraith, earth's uncreated dust,
Now signals with the flung-down fact of crystal,

Its stern-decreed geometry achieved,
Its pattern worked out to a T, its tip atom in place.

Where current rode the illimitable streaming
Too slow for any swirl to break the surface,
At that old, creeping, archetypal snail pace,
With none to note it, chaos inched back, worsted.
How landfall-like august form stands delivered!
Here's most diffuse most pointed, peaked, compacted,
Here's most amorphous grappled into jewel.

A Niche from the Blast

(Dell Concert)

Here in this lighted spot
On earth's dark surface as the night comes down,
And the bright westering star sinks toward its setting,
And color fades out, and the wide sky darkens,
The earth slow turning and the heavens wheeling—
As if for the first time, tonight I see
The firmament indeed is round about us,
We ride down very space, though we forget it.

And all about, the surge and storm and crying
Together of the instruments, man seeking
With passion for his true voice; while the husk
Of day falls off, and the startled night-bird quavers,
Pitting his scratch of sound against sound's tempest.

Now in this lighted hollow in the dark,
As in a momentary shelter found
Amid on-rushing suns, amid unknown
Encircling principalities and powers,
The dream comes out and sits upon the brow;
In a niche from the blast, the thousands are at peace—
Set free, made quick, at home with incandescence.

For One Without Fear

(M.C.W.)

Struck down. No warning; no quarter. As should be
For one without fear.
Knew she the end was toward, was on her? Did
Illumination grant a blinding minute?
Did ecstasy companion her (God grant),
Her old friend of the road at utmost need
Coming at call?

How now, unhoused, let abroad?
Dispersed past knowing, or still
Indestructibly one,
In what guise and whither now courses
Down what trajectory new
The unspent force that was she?

Left back in time
Along with us
The things she knew:
The fog, the sun, the desert, and the sea;
In the long-loved, swift-relinquished room
The shut book lying, and the Hittite seals.
With its dead-honest word
The worn and handled pebble speaks of her.

Anonymous Once

Seeing the risk of not being we men have all run,
Surveying the obstacles countered, the hurdles leaped over,
The pitfalls left headlong behind,
Must I not tremble to feel the sun on my shoulder?

The chances were all against it, but out of the dark
I was singled and came:
Anonymous once, elected into life
To a form of my own, no longer flotsam of dust
Adrift on the void, become particular,
A pointed star with a number and a name.

The Password

We have come to the edge of the continent; we know it.
We are through with solid ground.
The world of substance is dissolved in force,
In charge, in energies commensurate
With nothing that we know.
And *Humble* is the password of the wise.

Our power of search was greater than we guessed:
Men ran on tightrope hints
From here to there,
Brain wrested light from dark,
Five senses served us well.
Now we have need of ten,
Different and new;
For we conceive
A wall ahead,
Obdurate, granitic,
Adamant to tools worn out with whetting.
And *Humble* is the password of the wise.

This World

Early and late the backdrop is for joy;
The makings of wonder hang up on the air.
Fine, fine, like something seen from under the hand
On a morning in autumn, early, waits this world.

The heart sings out to see it hanging there
Half-apparition, marks it for its own,
Accepts the marvel freely as a child
That bends above the fadeless rock with laughter.

The forestage is the trouble; man made that,
And cannot blame another. (This I knew,
Returning to the changeless purpled mountain.)
Inept, impatient, like a fractious child

He tangles ropes and cords into a knot
That all but stops the play. Yet all the while
The makings of wonder hang up on the air,
Early and late the backdrop is for joy.

The Fundament Is Shifted

The call is for belief,
As once for doubt.
The old firm picture wavers
As if in water,
Like a thing off-centered.
The fundament is shifted by a hair's breadth;
What next we hear
May be the crack of doom—
Or be, instead,
Resurrection-horn blowing full A.

The physicist
In his high country of transparent landscape,
Who sees the mountains building, the chill growing
In the sun's flame-pit, dissolution snipping
Infinitesimal threads as grain flees grain
Under the beat of the wind and the rain and the sea—
He now, earth's cautious man,
Hazards a blinding guess that he is seeing
—Sprinkled apart, here, there, in the erst-failing cosmos—
Sun-creation raging in its might,
Rising to replace.

And others still,
Outrunning reach of dim-lit eye, make probe
Of modes of being more intense, and powers
Inchoate, dark, glimpsed to be lost again.

Men quail before such newness.
If less hinged upon it
We were less bleak-minded;
Would dare to trust our weight
On what is weightless,

And, like the astronaut,
With open eye
Step out on empty space as on a shelf,
Above the plane of falling.

And not fall.

New Poems (1970)

Under Sun-Beat

See earth's intractable carbon, stubborn set,
Seduced by ardors of the sun give over
Intransigence, and right about-face turning,
Side with the living, liven into leaf.

Not otherwise,
Under the sun-beat of great metaphor
Deluged and quickened, even stony fact
Breaks into green, and under swift compelling
Yields up to men its locked-in sustenance.

Breath-Air and Room

In the unlikeliest place,
In the innermost node of the twist,
May be breath-air and room
For being at large.

In the bore of the whirlpool, ringed round
With fury, waits dead rest for center;
In the fearful small room
In the eye of the hurricane, men
Ride the sky in an instant of stillness.

And some have dreamed,
In a wildness of daring,
Of life sweeping in from the windward of space
Unscathed in the meteor's pocket.

Martian Landscape

I think of the Martian landscape late delivered
To the eye of man by digits of a code
Reporting shades of grayness, darker, lighter,
In dull procession; in the end disclosing
To the rapt eye the unimagined craters.

—And I see a poem, word by word assembled
In markings down a page flash into code,
And bring in sightings of another landscape
No eye has seen before.

Alive This Night

I

This is what it is
To be alive; this night,
In the country within, in the dark of myself,
Whatever thought brushes is eyelashed with fire,
No edge but is lit, no cobble but glows.
Wakings beset; wherever I turn
Flarings play close within reach of my hand.

II

And outer and apart
Upshouldered from earth's floor
—Reared back upon themselves
Into bulks that eye
Can see and hand can touch
(Into stuff of stone,
A rock-face, see, a cliff!)—
The hooded energies
Unexhausted wait:
Hoarding atom fire,
Counting eons down,
Taut with chance of change.

III

This is the frame wherein
We live and walk this earth:
The galaxy and we therein
Sharing unspent charge within,
Quick with potential flame.

In Space-Time Aware—

Abysm past thinking on, chill
With menace cutting off words;
Yet yielding toehold to buds
And nooks to the younglings of birds.

Shaken by terror and joy
I see I belong where I am,
Here in the whelming abyss
As it were in the crook of an arm.

Index of Titles
and First Lines

Index of Titles and First Lines

PITT POETRY SERIES

COLOPHON

The poems in this book are set in
the Linotype version of Palatino, a typeface
designed by Hermann Zapf and aptly named for
the Italian scribe. The Linotype cutting is
slightly stronger than the other versions, but
it still retains the characteristic calligraphic
quality of the series.

The book was printed from the type by Heritage
Printers, Inc., and designed by Gary Gore.